FLYING TRAINING FOR THE PRIVATE PILOT LICENCE

MULTI ENGINE RATING

OAPA PRIVATE PILOT SYLLABUS (AEROPLANES)

The AOPA syllabus of training for the private pilot's licence as approved by the Civil Aviation Authority, details the areas of technical knowledge required in those subjects which are a mandatory part of the course.

In order to achieve conformity with this syllabus and assist the student in his learning task, a set of four training manuals has been specifically written to cover the knowledge requirements of the ground training section. The contents of these four manuals are listed below:

Manual One	Section 1	Air Legislation
	Section 2	Aviation Law, Flight Rules and Procedures
		Air Traffic Rules and Services
Manual Two	Section 3	Air Navigation
	Section 4	Aviation Meteorology
Manual Three	Section 5	Principles of Flight
	Section 6	Airframes and Aero Engines
	Section 7	Aircraft Airworthiness
	Section 8	Aircraft Instruments
Manual Four	Section 9	Specific Aircraft Type
	Section 10	Fire, First-Aid and Safety Equipment
	Section 11	Aeromedical Facts

Other manuals in this training series for instructors and students comprise:

> Flying Training for the Private Pilot Licence
> – Instructor Manual
> Flying Training for the Private Pilot Licence
> – Student Manual (Part One and Part Two)

Manuals are also available to cover the requirements of the:

> Night Rating
> Multi Engine Rating
> IMC Rating
> AOPA Aerobatic Certificate
> AOPA Radio Navigation Certificate

Additional manuals in this series will be published to cater for:

> Conversion onto Different Types of Aircraft
> (including Complex Types)
> Ditching and Survival Procedures

FLYING TRAINING FOR THE PRIVATE PILOT LICENCE
MULTI ENGINE RATING

R. D. CAMPBELL

COLLINS
8 Grafton Street, London W1

Collins Professional and Technical Books
William Collins Sons & Co. Ltd
8 Grafton Street, London W1X 3LA

First published in Great Britain by Aviation Training Publications Ltd 1980
Reprinted by Granada Publishing (original ISBN 0 246 11693 5) 1982
Reset and reprinted by Collins Professional and Technical Books 1986

Distributed in the United States of America
by Sheridan House, Inc.

Copyright © R.D. Campbell 1980, 1982, 1986

British Library Cataloguing in Publication Data
Campbell, R. D.
    Flying training for the private pilot licence.
    Multi engine rating
    1. Airplanes—Piloting   2. Private flying
    I. Title   II. Aircraft Owners & Pilots Association
    629.132'5217   TL710

ISBN 0-00-383352-6

Typeset by Columns of Reading
Printed and bound in Great Britain by
Mackays of Chatham Ltd, Kent

Nothing in this manual must be taken as superseding the legislation, rules,
regulations, procedures and information contained in the Air Navigation Order,
the Air Navigation (General) Regulations, Rules of the Air and Air Traffic
Control Regulations, the UK Air Pilot, NOTAMS, Aeronautical Information
Circulars, or the recommendations, restrictions, limitations and operating
procedures published in aircraft, engines or systems manuals and Certificates of
Airworthiness, or any Civil Air Publication or similar document published by
the Civil Aviation Authority.

Contents

Flight Syllabus – Long Briefings

Flight Syllabus – Flight Demonstrations

Acknowledgements

Grateful acknowledgements are made to the Civil Aviation Authority, for permitting reproduction of certain material in this Manual.

Acknowledgements are also made to those members of the Civil Aviation Authority and Aircraft Manufacturers, to Mr J Jones MA Cantab, Dr R G James ACGI, BSc, PhD Cantab, and to those members of the AOPA Instructor Committee and Panel of Examiners, for their advice and helpful suggestions, all of which formed an important contribution to this Training Manual.

Study Guide

Stage 1
    Start by studying from page 19 Technical Subjects, UK Air Legislation, through to page 31, The Air Navigation (General) Regulations.
    Read through the guidance notes at the beginning of the Progress Tests section and:
        Complete Quiz No. 1, page Q5.
    Note: Provision for entering the answers is either integrated on the appropriate question page or contained at the end of each quiz.

Stage 2
    Study from page 32, Flight on Asymmetric Power, to page 46, Thrust and Rudder Side Force Couples.
    Complete Quiz No. 2, page Q11.

Stage 3
    Study from page 47, Control in Asymmetric Power Flight, to page 84, Accelerate–Stop Distance Considerations.
    Complete Quiz No. 3, page Q14.

Stage 4
    Study from page 85, Long Briefing, Part 1 Normal Flight, through to page 97.
    Complete Quiz No. 4, page Q19.

Stage 5
    Study from page 98, Long Briefing, Part 1 Normal Flight, through to page 108.
    Complete Quiz No. 5, page Q21.

Stage 6
    Study from page 109, Long Briefing, Part 1 Normal Flight, through to page 116.
    Complete Quiz No. 6, page Q22.

Stage 7
Study from page 117, Long Briefing, Part 2 Asymmetric Flight, through to page 124.
Complete Quiz No. 7, page Q24.

Stage 8
Study from page 125, Long Briefing, Part 2 Asymmetric Flight, through to page 133.
Complete Quiz No. 8, page Q28.

Stage 9
Study from page 134, Long Briefing, Part 2 Asymmetric Flight, through to page 148.
Complete Quiz No. 9, page Q32.
Note: Pages 146–8 concern the operation of *Centre-Line Thrust* aircraft. The holder of a Multi Engine Rating is permitted to fly these aircraft and should therefore study the information contained on these pages.

Flight Instruction

AMENDMENT LIST No.	DATE INCORPORATED	SIGNATURE

Applicability of this Manual and Suitability of Training Aircraft

The 'Flight Demonstrations' contained in the OAPA Syllabus and this Manual apply only to those multi engined aeroplanes which are able to go round again from an approach on asymmetric power, climb to a normal visual circuit height in a reasonable time and distance, and complete a circuit and landing under asymmetric power in standard local atmospheric conditions at maximum or near maximum authorised weight, when flown by a normally competent pilot.

In the UK these will include twin engined aeroplanes certificated in Performance Group C and some in Performance Group E. Courses for the Group B Rating for inclusion on a Private Pilot Licence, and courses for the multi engine qualification on a Flying Instructors Rating, should be given only on aeroplanes that can meet these standards of performance.

LOW PERFORMANCE MULTI ENGINED AEROPLANES

Other multi engined aeroplanes that cannot achieve at least Performance Group C standards must be regarded as if they were single engined types.

Thus should an engine fail on an aircraft of this type at any time during flight, the correct procedure is to adopt and maintain a safe gliding speed and make a forced landing according to the standard procedures for single engined aeroplanes using the available power to reduce the rate of descent.

No attempt should be made to return to an aerodrome using asymmetric power unless this can be accomplished as part of a standard or near standard forced landing. It should be noted, furthermore, that even then, these aeroplanes may present handling problems when flown with asymmetric thrust if directional control is difficult for whatever reason.

Definitions

TAS The true speed of the aeroplane relative to undisturbed air.

EAS Equivalent air speed. TAS $(\rho/\rho_0)^{\frac{1}{2}}$ or TAS $(\sigma)^{\frac{1}{2}}$

IAS Indicated air speed. The readings of the pitot-static air speed indicator as installed in the aeroplane, corrected only for the instrument error.

V_a The design manoeuvring speed, EAS.

V_{fe} Wing flaps extended speed. A maximum speed, IAS, with wing flaps in a prescribed extended position.

V_{le} Landing gear extended speed. The maximum speed, IAS, at which the aeroplane is suitable to be flown safely with the landing gear extended.

V_{lo} Landing gear operating speed. A maximum speed, IAS, at which it is safe to extend or to retract the landing gear.

V_{mca} The minimum control speed, EAS, with the critical engine made inoperative during take-off (see pages 50–51).

V_{ne} The never exceed speed, IAS.

V_{no} The normal operating limit speed, IAS.

V_{s1} A stalling speed (or if no stalling speed is obtainable, the minimum steady flight speed), EAS, with the aeroplane in the configuration appropriate to the case under consideration.

V_{so} A stalling speed (or if no stalling speed is obtainable, a minimum steady flight speed), EAS, with wing flaps in the landing setting.

V_2 The take-off safety speed, EAS for flight requirements, IAS for operating information. A speed used in the determination of take-off performance.

V_{yse} The best rate of climb airspeed on one engine.

V_{sse} The best angle of climb airspeed on one engine. (See pages 57–8.)

Conversion to Twin Engined Aircraft

Instructor's Guide

Before attempting to convert a pilot to multi engine aircraft, an instructor must be approved to do so and be competent on the particular aircraft type. The conversion course must then follow a syllabus which has been approved by the Civil Aviation Authority and a statement to this effect, signed by the instructor who conducted the training must be made on the pilot's application form for the grant of a Group 'B' Rating.

The actual training is divided into two distinct phases, the first of which involves flight with all engines operating normally, and the second, asymmetric flight. In the case of Centre-Line Thrust aircraft, the second phase will involve the handling and performance aspects of operating the aircraft on one engine, and the demonstrations and practice must also include single engined flight using each engine in turn.

In this manual the total flight training has been divided into 6 separate instructional sequences. These are for planning guidance only, and can be varied according to the operational requirements. A further point to mention is that whereas the exact sequence and content of these Long Briefings and Flight Demonstrations are not necessarily the only way to carry out multi engine instruction, adherence to the general format and sequences contained herein will clearly assist the student if he is studying from the complementary AOPA Student Manual for the Multi Engine Rating.

Instructional points of particular note are outlined as follows:

The objective of flying instruction is to ensure that the student can *operate an aircraft safely and with confidence*. To this end it is just as important in terms of efficiency that the cost of the training should not be allowed to outweigh the importance of ensuring that the student obtains sufficient practice at handling the aircraft under normal conditions before he is trained in the asymmetric or single engined flight procedures. Insufficient practice at handling the aircraft in normal manoeuvres will adversely affect the student's rate of progress in handling more difficult situations, i.e.

asymmetric flight, thereby undermining his motivation and confidence.

Due to the greater complexity of operating a twin engined aircraft the need for unhurried use of checklists will be a requirement, and care should be taken to ensure that the student follows the checklist item by item and does not use his memory to speed up the rate at which the checks are carried out.

Emergency procedures should, however, be learned so that they can be initially performed from memory, and once the situation is under immediate control the checklist should be used as an *aide-mémoire* to ensure that all the necessary procedures have been completed.

The student must be clearly briefed on the ground and reminded in the air about the use of 'Touch Drills' when practising emergencies. Unnecessary accidents may occur when the student pilot selects and moves the wrong lever or switch, before the instructor is able to stop him from doing so. This type of hazard is greatest when insufficient time is available for the instructor to take corrective action, or to remedy the mistake, e.g. during engine failure practice after take-off.

The instructor must be completely conversant with the normal and emergency operating procedures of the particular training aircraft. Considerable reference to the Flight/Owner's Manual/Pilot's Operating Handbook must be made during the course of instruction, because, due to the many differences between twin engined aircraft and their associated systems, it is extremely difficult for any training manual to cover the individual operating aspects of the many light twin engined aircraft available for training.

Additional reference material which must be available during the course are the Air Navigation Order, Air Navigation (General) Regulations, Specimen Weight and Performance Manuals Groups C and E, and when possible, Section K of the British Civil Airworthiness Requirements.

Multi engined aircraft have significantly higher noise levels than single engined aircraft and instructors must remain acutely aware of this fact when operating out of aerodromes in the vicinity of populated areas. It must be emphasised to all instructors that today the Environmental Associations are very quick to complain about aircraft noise and this has a tendency to increase flying restrictions.

Therefore, in order to minimise the effects of aircraft noise on the public and reduce the frequency of complaints, instructors must ensure that they apply self imposed noise abatement procedures consistent with the safe operation of their aircraft and compliance with ATC procedures. This can often be accomplished by avoiding flight at lower altitudes over populated areas, by reducing power more quickly after take-off, and adopting steeper approaches when noise-sensitive areas exist adjacent to the particular aerodrome.

PRE-FLIGHT PREPARATION

The instructor must ensure that the student understands the effect of incorrect Weight and Balance, and the fact that both the weight and the centre of gravity will change during flight as fuel is consumed. This is particularly so when rear seat passengers and baggage are carried.

Weight and Performance is another area which may be new to the pilot who has only operated in single engined aircraft. Therefore due consideration must be given to this aspect. The student must also be fully acquainted with the aircraft documentation including the Flight/Owner's Manual/Pilot's Operating Handbook, the Certificate of Airworthiness and maintenance records.

PRE-FLIGHT CHECKS

The external and internal checks should be done according to the checklist for type. Two specific areas of importance are the checking of baggage and cabin doors to ensure they are fully closed and secure, and the seating position which must be very carefully checked to ensure that the student can apply full rudder travel without difficulty.

With reference to cabin doors, many accidents have occurred without warning due to baggage or cabin doors opening in flight, particularly just after take-off. Ensure the student is aware of the problems of doors opening in flight. For example, an open cabin door will rarely prevent the pilot from controlling the aircraft adequately and landing safely, provided he does not panic or make an ill-considered decision. However, the opening of baggage doors located in the aircraft nose section can be very hazardous during flight, and extreme care must be taken during the pre-flight check to ensure they are securely closed and fastened.

The ability to apply maximum rudder movement is particularly related to an engine failure situation in conventional twin engined aircraft, rather than the spin recovery procedure as with single engined types, though this latter consideration is always important regardless of the aeroplane being flown.

One difficulty in relation to seat or rudder adjustment is that a coupled nosewheel, due to its design, can often make it impossible to determine whether the student can apply full rudder whilst the aircraft is on the ground. Therefore this will have to be checked as soon as convenient during practice asymmetric conditions when airborne, and the seat or adjustable rudder position noted for future reference during pre-flight checks.

Bearing in mind the increased aerodynamic loads on multi engine aircraft, another aspect relating to use of the controls which must be carefully watched for during training is the need for a pilot to have the physical strength to apply full rudder under asymmetric conditions at low speed. Also the ability to cope with other situations, e.g. a runaway electric trimmer. Either or both of these conditions could prove to be outside the physical capabilities of some persons.

In the event that a candidate for a multi engine rating is unable to cope physically with certain in-flight situations in a specific aircraft, the training must be discontinued and conducted on another less physically demanding type.

TAXYING

Due to the larger wing span, the instructor will need to monitor the student's actions carefully when in the vicinity of parking areas and obstructions. The greater inertia and tendency for higher taxying speeds may also lead a student into the habit of riding the brakes in an effort to control speed. Additional alertness will also be required when sharp bends occur on taxiways, because of the wider track of the landing gear.

TAKE-OFF

In this manual, Sequence 3 of Part 1 of the Long Briefings and Flight Demonstrations covers the period of training on the circuit, but it will clearly be of benefit to introduce the student to these operations from the first flight onwards. Therefore, Sequence 1 of Part 1 introduces some of the aspects which relate to the take-off, circuit and landing, and Sequence 3 should be used for the consolidation of previously learned procedures, and demonstration and practise of the remaining items.

It will be advisable to ensure the pilot understands the purpose of reviewing such speeds as V_{mca}, V_2, and V_{yse}, from the beginning of his flight training.

EMERGENCIES

Ensure the student spends sufficient time on the ground practising the various emergency situations which could occur during flight. The procedures to be employed in relation to fire, failure of the aircraft services and systems, etc., must be obtained from the Flight/Owner's Manual/Pilot's Operating Handbook for the particular type and model.

FLIGHT ON ASYMMETRIC POWER

'On any occasion when an engine is shut down in flight or an engine failure is simulated at a low height, the flight safety margins are automatically reduced. Further to this, and because of the purpose of asymmetric power training, a significant proportion of single engined training is spent in demonstrating and practising emergency procedures which involve critical manoeuvres whilst the aircraft is near the ground.

These circumstances will lead to an increased demand on the skill and competence of the pilot, therefore the multi rated instructor will need to achieve and maintain a high level of technical knowledge and flying competence on each multi engined aircraft in which he gives this training. To be found wanting in either of these qualities or lacking in alertness for errors will nullify the very purpose upon which flying instruction is based.'

Priority must be given to the various asymmetric exercises to ensure that the student has sufficient practice and achieves a high standard of competence in handling these situations. Frequent practice, resulting in an unflurried approach to the procedures following an engine failure, will be considered a necessary requirement. The student will also have to display a high standard of airmanship in stress situations, to demonstrate that he is capable of exercising the privileges of a multi engine rating.

Demonstrations which involve actual feathering must be carried out at a safe altitude, normally above 3000′ agl., and within a safe distance from an aerodrome, so that in the event of partial or total failure of the operating engine, there will be time to rectify the situation either by unfeathering the other engine or by adopting a glide to reach an aerodrome safely.

When demonstrating the effects of engine failure and the procedures to be adopted, it will be advisable to simulate partial, as well as complete, engine failure from various flight conditions, e.g. level, climbing and descending flight. Many engine failures occur due to mismanagement of the fuel system and this aspect should be stressed.

When covering the method of maintaining control during asymmetric flight, the effects of incorrect use of rudder and ailerons, i.e. too little rudder and too much aileron, should (when permitted on type) also be demonstrated to illustrate the adverse results of relying upon ailerons as a primary means of retaining direction.

When simulating engine failure after take-off, extreme care must be exercised to ensure that adequate airspeed and altitude have been gained prior to closing a throttle. It will also be vital to monitor the student's actions in relation to his 'Touch Drills' to avoid inadvertent selection of the wrong engine controls.

In relation to handling the aircraft in the circuit, a common fault is for pilots to gradually and unnecessarily lose height on the downwind leg when on asymmetric power. Stress the importance of maintaining circuit height until the aircraft is established on the base leg.

The use of *Asymmetric Committal Height* is to ensure that time and height is available to carry out a safe *Go Around* on asymmetric power. If the student goes round again from this height but loses height during the initial process of cleaning up the aircraft and establishing V_{yse}, this must not necessarily be considered as a poor performance. The object of stating an asymmetric committal height is to allow for a possible loss of height during that period when the aircraft is being cleaned up and V_{yse} established.

CENTRE-LINE THRUST AIRCRAFT

Due to the lack of asymmetric thrust and drag, these aircraft are more easily controlled if an engine fails during the take-off run or in flight. The single engine operational aspects are therefore mainly confined to the use of the correct emergency procedures and the problems of a significantly reduced performance.

It must nevertheless be appreciated that one natural difficulty for the pilot will lie in the fact that although the engines are in line with one another, fore and aft, the engine controls are normally laid out as for a conventional aircraft, i.e. in a line athwart the throttle quadrant. This difference in disposition between the engines and their controls can more easily cause confusion when selecting an engine control, particularly when the pilot is under the stress which results from one engine failing.

The need to lead with the throttle of the rear engine when commencing a take-off is also an important consideration, as this method of power application will more quickly determine the integrity of the operation of the rear engine, as this power unit is not visible to the pilot.

Another important point to bear in mind is that some Centre-Line Thrust aircraft may only have one hydraulic pump to operate the landing gear. Therefore if the engine which drives this pump fails shortly after take-off and the landing gear is then selected up, a situation would occur where the residual pressure in the system will be insufficient to complete the retraction cycle.

In these circumstances the large amount of drag caused by the landing gear doors opening out from the fuselage could cause a critical situation if the aircraft is at low height and low speed. It will therefore be very important to ensure that the student appreciates this fact.

Conversion to Twin Engined Aircraft

Student's Guide

The operating versatility, efficiency and environmental safety aspects obtainable from small modern multi engined aircraft have played an important part in the increased number of pilots obtaining multi engine Ratings.

Nevertheless it must also be clearly appreciated from the outset of your twin engine conversion training that there is an increased need for you to study and understand the various differences in flight characteristics and operating procedures between twin engined and single engined aircraft.

The development of good judgement and the use of correct procedures can only come through knowledge and ability, which in turn can only be achieved by study and practice. In this respect a thorough knowledge of the aircraft operating procedures in both normal and abnormal conditions, as detailed in the particular Flight/ Owner's Manual/Pilot's Operating Handbook for type, and the associated regulations laid down in the Air Navigation Order, and Air Navigation (General) Regulations, will enable you to handle more safely any contingency which may arise during flight.

The purpose of this manual is to enable you to cover the requirements as outlined in the AOPA Multi Engine Rating Syllabus. A thorough grasp of the knowledge and procedures covered in the following pages will enable you to develop the greater competence needed to fly a multi engined aircraft safely, and the information contained in the Technical Subjects section should be studied prior to the commencement of your flight training.

The object of the Long Briefing and Flight Demonstration sections is to prepare you for the appropriate stages of your flight training and as such they should be studied prior to undertaking the particular flight sequence to which they refer. In this way you will be better prepared to understand the purpose of the flight exercise, and so obtain greater benefit from your flight practice.

It should nevertheless be appreciated that due to differences between the various twin engined aircraft available for training, your instructor may not follow the precise pattern of the Flight Demonstrations outlined in this manual.

A final important point concerns the added noise factor of multi engined aircraft, and the increasing emphasis at the present time in minimising the effect of aircraft noise on the public.

All pilots must therefore give consideration to this environmental aspect, and where possible apply self-imposed noise abatement procedures, provided always that they are consistent with the safe operation of the aircraft, and ATC procedures.

This will mean avoiding or minimising your flight duration over populated areas at low altitudes, and where it is possible with safety, employing steeper approaches to landing and/or reducing power a little earlier during the take-off, climb out period, whenever the path of the aircraft is such as will take it over populated areas.

Weight and Performance is another area which may be new to the pilot who has only operated in single engined aircraft. Therefore due consideration must be given to this aspect. You must also be fully acquainted with the aircraft documentation including the Flight/Owner's Manual/Pilot's Operating Handbook, the Certificate of Airworthiness and maintenance records.

PRE-FLIGHT CHECKS

The external and internal checks should be done according to the checklist for type. Two specific areas of importance are the checking of baggage and cabin doors to ensure they are fully closed and secure, and the seating position which must be very carefully checked to ensure that you can apply full rudder travel without difficulty.

With reference to cabin doors, many accidents have occurred without warning due to baggage or cabin doors opening in flight, particularly just after take-off. The degree of hazard varies depending on the type and position of the door, for example, an open cabin door will rarely prevent the pilot from controlling the aircraft adequately and landing safely, provided he does not panic or make an ill-considered decision. However, the opening of baggage doors located in the aircraft nose section can be very hazardous during flight, and extreme care must be taken during the pre-flight check to ensure they are securely closed and fastened.

The ability to apply maximum rudder movement is particularly related to an engine failure situation in conventional twin engined aircraft, rather than the spin recovery procedure as with single engined types, though this latter consideration is always important regardless of the aeroplane being flown.

One difficulty in relation to seat or rudder adjustment is that a coupled nosewheel, due to its design, can often make it impossible to determine whether a pilot can apply full rudder whilst the aircraft is on the ground. Therefore this will have to be checked as soon as convenient during practice asymmetric conditions when airborne, and the seat or adjustable rudder position noted for future reference during pre-flight checks.

Bearing in mind the increased aerodynamic loads on multi engine aircraft, another aspect relating to use of the controls which must be carefully watched for during training is the need for a pilot to have the physical strength to apply full rudder under asymmetric conditions at low speed. Also the ability to cope with other situations, e.g. a runaway electric trimmer. Either or both of these conditions could prove to be outside the physical capabilities of some persons.

In the event that a candidate for a multi engine rating is unable to cope physically with certain in-flight situations in a specific aircraft, the training must be discontinued and conducted on another less physically demanding type.

TAXYING

Due to the larger wing span, you will need to take greater care when manoeuvring in the vicinity of parking areas and obstructions. The greater inertia and tendency for higher taxying speeds may also lead you into the habit of riding the brakes in an effort to control speed. Additional alertness will also be required when sharp bends occur on taxiways, because of the wider track of the landing gear.

TAKE-OFF

In this manual, Sequence 3 of Part 1 of the Long Briefings and Flight Demonstrations covers the period of training on the circuit, but it will clearly be of benefit to introduce you to these operations from the first flight onwards. Therefore, Sequence 1 of Part 1 introduces some of the aspects which relate to the take-off, circuit and landing, and Sequence 3 should be used for the consolidation of previously learned procedures, and demonstration and practice of the remaining items.

It will be advisable for you to understand the purpose of reviewing such speeds as V_{mca}, V_2, and V_{yse}, from the beginning of your flight training.

EMERGENCIES

The pilot will need to spend sufficient time on the ground practising the various emergency situations which could occur during flight. The procedures to be employed in relation to fire, failure of the aircraft services and systems, etc., must be obtained from the Flight/Owner's

Manual/Pilot's Operating Handbook for the particular type and model.

FLIGHT ON ASYMMETRIC POWER

'On any occasion when an engine is shut down in flight or an engine failure is simulated at a low height, the flight safety margins are automatically reduced. Further to this, and because of the purpose of asymmetric power training, a significant proportion of single engined training is spent in demonstrating and practising emergency procedures which involve critical manoeuvres whilst the aircraft is near the ground.

These circumstances will lead to an increased demand on the skill and competence of the pilot, thus there is a need to achieve and maintain a high level of technical knowledge and flying competence on each multi engined aircraft you fly. To be found wanting in either of these qualities or lacking in alertness for errors will nullify the very purpose upon which flying instruction is given.'

Priority will be given to the various asymmetric exercises to ensure that you have sufficient practice and achieve a high standard of competence in handling these situations. Frequent practice, resulting in an unflurried approach to the procedures following an engine failure, will be considered a necessary requirement. You will also have to display a high standard of airmanship in stress situations, to demonstrate that you are capable of exercising the privileges of a multi engine rating.

Demonstrations which involve actual feathering must be carried out at a safe altitude, normally above 3000' agl., and within a safe distance from an aerodrome, so that in the event of partial or total failure of the operating engine, there will be time to rectify the situation either by unfeathering the other engine or by adopting a glide to reach an aerodrome safely.

When demonstrating the effects of engine failure and the procedures to be adopted, it will be advisable to simulate partial, as well as complete, engine failure from various flight conditions, e.g. level, climbing and descending flight. Many engine failures occur due to mismanagement of the fuel system and this aspect should be stressed.

When covering the method of maintaining control during asymmetric flight, the effects of incorrect use of rudder and ailerons, i.e. too little rudder and too much aileron, should (when permitted on type) also be demonstrated to illustrate the adverse results of relying upon ailerons as a primary means of retaining direction.

When simulating engine failure after take-off, extreme care must be exercised to ensure that adequate airspeed and altitude have been gained prior to closing a throttle. It will also be vital to monitor your actions in relation to 'Touch Drills' to avoid touching the wrong engine controls.

In relation to handling the aircraft in the circuit, a common fault is for pilots to gradually and unnecessarily lose height on the downwind leg when on asymmetric power. The importance of maintaining circuit height until the aircraft is established on the base leg is paramount.

The use of *Asymmetric Committal Height* is to ensure that time and height is available to carry out a safe *Go Around* on asymmetric power. If you go round again from this height but lose height during the initial process of cleaning up the aircraft and establishing V_{yse}, this is not necessarily considered a poor performance. The object of stating an asymmetric committal height is to allow for a possible loss of height during that period when the aircraft is being cleaned up and V_{yse} established.

CENTRE-LINE THRUST AIRCRAFT

Due to the lack of asymmetric thrust and drag, these aircraft are more easily controlled if an engine fails during the take-off run or in flight. The single engine operational aspects are therefore mainly confined to the use of the correct emergency procedures and the problems of a significantly reduced performance.

It must nevertheless be appreciated that one natural difficulty for the pilot will lie in the fact that although the engines are in line with one another, fore and aft, the engine controls are normally laid out as for a conventional aircraft, i.e. in a line athwart the throttle quadrant. This difference in disposition between the engines and their controls can more easily cause confusion when selecting an engine control, particularly when the pilot is under the stress which results from one engine failing.

The need to lead with the throttle of the rear engine when commencing a take-off is also an important consideration, as this method of power application will more quickly determine the integrity of the operation of the rear engine, as this power unit is not visible to the pilot.

Another important point to bear in mind is that some Centre-Line Thrust aircraft may only have one hydraulic pump to operate the landing gear. Therefore if the engine which drives this pump fails shortly after take-off and the landing gear is then selected up, a situation would occur where the residual pressure in the system will be insufficient to complete the retraction cycle.

In these circumstances the large amount of drag caused by the landing gear doors opening out from the fuselage could cause a critical situation if the aircraft is at low height and low speed. It will therefore be very important to ensure that you appreciate this fact.

Introduction

A multi engined aircraft provides factors of performance, load capability, range, and safety which are greater than those normally achieved by single engined aircraft.

The increased power derived from a twin engined aeroplane will nevertheless bring with it added complexity in terms of aircraft operation and performance, and a greater need for a pilot to achieve and maintain a wider range of competence in pre-flight planning, flying techniques and decisions, than those required by less complex aircraft.

The purpose of this manual is to meet the training requirements laid own in the multi engine rating course and it conforms to the layout and sequence of the AOPA Syllabus as approved by the UK Civil Aviation Authority.

The content of the following sections adheres to this Syllabus to the depth of knowledge required by a pilot who aspires to achieve competence and safety when operating a twin engined aeroplane within the privileges of the Private Pilot Licence.

The manual is divided into the following Sections:

Ground Syllabus – Technical
                  Subjects
Flight Syllabus – Long Briefings
                 – Flight
                   Demonstrations
Progress Tests

The Technical Subjects Section covers to the necessary depth the principles involved in operating a twin engined aircraft both in normal and asymmetric flight.

The practical aspects of twin engined aircraft training are covered in the sections entitled 'Long Briefings' and 'Flight Demonstrations'.

This layout and sequence are designed to simplify the pilot's studies, and aid the development of those skills which must necessarily be acquired for the issue of a multi engine rating – in the UK this is known as a Group B Rating.

Accident records support the fact that pilots who risk flying unfamiliar aircraft without proper conversion training expose themselves and others to unnecessary danger.

There is no substitute for proper conversion training, and the satisfaction and greater safety which result from it more than repay the cost and effort. A more cogent consideration is that the law requires competence in handling the aircraft and it is a first requirement in the rules of captaincy. Safe handling of an in-flight emergency is not a question of luck, although good luck always helps, but rather the result of sound training and frequent practice. There is no substitute for this, not in fact, nor by the exercise of responsible thought.

Pilots who undertake proper conversion training, who obtain a sound knowledge of their aircraft handling characteristics, systems and operating procedures, coupled with recency practice in coping with abnormal situations, and who implement methodical pre-flight preparation, will achieve a greater satisfaction and safety, both of which are vital requirements for any responsible pilot.

GROUND SYLLABUS

Technical Subjects

UK Air Legislation

The purpose of CAA regulations implemented through legislation is to provide certain basic minimum standards of safety. These cannot be achieved without some form of aircraft certification, pilot licensing, and standard operating procedures. Pilots who progress from single engined aeroplanes to multi engined aeroplanes must appreciate that the additional complexity of operating a more complicated aircraft also brings with it the need for additional pilot disciplines and pre-flight preparation.

For example, a multi engined aircraft will normally have a far greater variety of available loading options in relation to fuel, passengers, and baggage, and this will mean that weight and balance calculations will be more complex and will also be required more frequently during pre-flight planning.

Another example is apparent in considering take-off and climb performance of a multi engined aeroplane, in that, although added flexibility and safety is achieved by having more than one engine, this flexibility and safety can be completely negated if insufficient distance is available for the take-off and initial climb out, especially in the event of the failure of one engine during this period.

PRE-FLIGHT ACTION BY COMMANDER OF AIRCRAFT

The Air Navigation Order specifies the pre-flight actions that should be covered prior to every flight, and although many training flights may not require all these to be completed in detail they nevertheless indicate those which are considered necessary, prior to any flight.

The commander of an aircraft must satisfy himself before the aircraft takes off:

AIR NAVIGATION ORDER

- That he is properly licensed to act as pilot in command for the period of the flight.
- That the flight can safely be made, taking into account the latest information available as to the route and aerodromes to be used, the weather reports and forecasts available, and any alternative courses of action which can be adopted in case the flight cannot be completed as planned, e.g. diverting to an alternate airfield, or turning back to the departure airfield.
- That all the equipment required for the flight (including radio if applicable) is carried and in a fit condition for use.
- That the aircraft is in every way fit for the intended flight, and the required documentation, e.g. Certificate of Airworthiness and Certificate of Release (or equivalent maintenance document), are valid for the period of flight.
- That the load carried by the aircraft is so distributed and secured that it may safely be carried on the intended flight.
- That sufficient fuel, oil, and where applicable engine coolant, are carried and that a safe margin has been allowed for such contingencies as getting lost, or having to divert.
- That due regard has been observed in relation to the aircraft's performance in respect of being able to safely take-off and land within the available distance at the departure and destination airfields (including selected alternatives) and to maintaining a safe height on the intended or alternative route.

Although all these items are included in the syllabus for the basic private pilot licence for single engined aeroplanes and should therefore have been covered in a pilot's initial course of training, it is appropriate to briefly cover in this manual the

> Approved AOPA Syllabus for the
>
> # Private Pilot Licence
> (Aeroplanes)
> and associated Ratings

application of these considerations to multi engined aircraft operations.

PILOT LICENSING

That the pilot is properly licensed ...

When a licence is first issued it will contain an Aircraft Rating page which lists the groups of aircraft the holder is entitled to fly. For private pilots the various types of aeroplanes are divided into three Groups as follows:

Group A   All types of single engined aeroplanes of which the maximum total weight authorised does not exceed 5700 kg.

Group B   Certain types of aeroplanes having two or more engines of which the maximum total weight authorised does not exceed 5700 kg.

Group C   Individual types of aeroplanes of which the maximum total weight authorised exceeds 5700 kg or are considered to be of a complex nature.

Privileges of the Aircraft Rating

A licence cannot be issued without including a Certificate of Test and an Aircraft Rating for at least one of the above Groups of aeroplanes. Once a group or type has been entered in an Aircraft Rating it will not normally be removed, but the entitlement to fly an aeroplane and exercise the privileges of a private pilot within the group, or of the type listed, will be dependent upon a certain minimum flight time within a particular period being carried out by the holder of the licence in that group, or in the case of Group 'C', in the specific type.

AIRCRAFT RATING-AEROPLANES			
The holder of this licence, is entitled to exercise its privileges either as pilot in command or as co-pilot of aeroplanes as specified below.			
Landplanes Seaplanes Amphibians	Group A Group B		
Self Launching Motor Gliders			
Group C			

Initial Test for the Group B Rating

A specific course of training is required to obtain a Group B Rating. This course consists of a minimum of 6 hours flying and 7 hours ground instruction. When this has been satisfactorily completed a Flight Test and an Oral Examination must be given by an authorised examiner. If a candidate is applying for the initial issue of a Private Pilot Licence with an Aircraft Rating in Group B, the written Technical Examination Aeroplanes, Part 1 and the private pilot Aviation Law, Navigation and Meteorology Examinations must also be completed.

The Flight Test

This will include all the normal flight procedures which are covered in the flight test for Group A (single engined) aeroplanes and those emergency procedures applicable to the specific group and type on which the test is conducted. Full details of the items in which a candidate for a Group B Rating will be tested are shown in Fig. 1.

Name of Applicant:				
Aircraft Type(s)	Registration letters	Place of Test	Duration of Test	Date of Test

AEROPLANES – GROUP 'B'				
PREPARATION FOR FLIGHT	Date	STALLING		Date
Weather suitability		Checks before stalling		
Aeroplane documents check		Recovery from developed stall		
Personal Equipment check		Recovery at the incipient stage		
Weight and balance – calculate		In approach configuration – Sim. Finals turn		
Weight and performance – calculate		AIRFIELD APPROACH PROCEDURES		
Fuel and oil state		CIRCUIT PROCEDURE		
Aeroplane acceptance		APPROACH AND LANDING		
Booking out – ATC		Pre-landing checks (vital actions)		
Pre-flight inspection		Checks after landing		
STARTING, TAXYING AND POWER		Powered approach		
Pre-start checks		Bad weather circuit, short field		
Post-start checks		Cross-wind landing		
Taxying techniques		Assessment of cross-wind component		
Power checks		MISSED APPROACH PROCEDURE		
TAKE-OFF		SIMULATED EMERGENCIES		
Pre-take-off check (vital actions)		Engine fire in the air/on the ground		
During and post-take-off checks		Cabin fire in the air/on the ground		
Normal take-off		OTHER SIMULATED EMERGENCIES		
Cross-wind take-off		ENGINES AND SYSTEMS HANDLING		
Assessment of cross-wind component		AIRMANSHIP – AWARENESS		
AERODROME DEPARTURE PROCEDURES		Look-out		
CLIMBING		Positioning – restricted air space, hazards, weather		
STRAIGHT AND LEVEL FLIGHT		ATC liaison		
DESCENDING WITH POWER/FLAP		Aerodrome discipline		
TURNING		ACTION AFTER FLIGHT		
Level		Engine shut down		
Climbing		Parking and securing aeroplane		
Descending		Recording of flight details		
At high angles of bank		*NOTE: Feathering should only be done at a height which would enable engine power to be restored and safe flight continued should the other engine fail.		
UNUSUAL ATTITUDES				
Recovery from a spiral drive				
Recovery from steep climbing turn				
FLIGHT WITH ASYMMETRIC POWER				
*Feathering and unfeathering if permitted by Flight Manual		Simulated engine failure after take-off at or above safety speed		
Procedure for engine failure in the cruise		Approach and overshoot one engine at zero thrust		
All normal manoeuvres with one engine inoperative. Compliance with recommended speeds.		Approach and land one engine at zero thrust		
Determination of minimum control speeds		Use of Asymmetric Committal Height (Decision Height).		

Fig. 1

When the required flying and ground training, including flight test and oral examination, have been completed, the application form, together with the candidate's log book and aircraft Rating card, should be sent to the CAA (FCL3).

Maintaining the Privileges of the Aircraft Rating

At the end of every 13 months period, during the life of the licence, regardless of his age or flight experience, the holder of a private pilot licence will be required to submit his licence and personal flying log book to an authorised examiner for a check of his flying experience over that period. To renew the privileges of the Aircraft Rating (i.e. to retain the right to fly the aircraft listed therein), the licence holder is required either to obtain a certain minimum amount of flying

experience during the 13 months period, or alternatively, to pass a flight test at the end of the period.

The minimum flying experience required in each 13 month period to maintain the privileges of the Group B Rating is as follows:

5 hours experience as pilot in command (a maximum of 2 hours dual flying instruction can count towards this total) of an aircraft of the same class as that which the pilot wishes to fly, of which at least one flight in command and unsupervised, i.e. not pic u/s, shall have been made in a multi engined aircraft.

WEATHER, ROUTE AND AERODROMES TO BE USED
That the flight can safely be made in relation to the route, aerodromes, weather information . . .

The greater distances which can be flown in a multi engined aircraft lead to the possibility of the pilot planning stage lengths of well over 1000 miles or more. In addition to this, many such aircraft are equipped with an oxygen or cabin pressurisation system, and are sometimes certificated for flight over 30 000'.

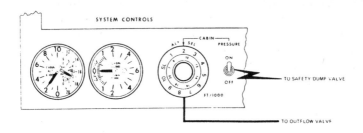

Both these factors give the aircraft greater flexibility of operation than is possible in most single engined aircraft. Consequently the pilot may be exposed to a wider variety of routes and weather situations than he has been before. Additional care must therefore be exercised to ensure that he does not over-reach his own capabilities in planning longer flights, or in conducting flights at higher altitudes.

There will also be a need for greater care in obtaining up-to-date weather information. Multi engined aircraft also generally require longer take-off and landing distances, so the take-off and landing distances available at those aerodromes to be used en route or selected as alternatives must be ascertained.

AIRCRAFT EQUIPMENT
That all equipment required for the flight is serviceable . . .

A larger amount and a wider variety of equipment is usually

installed in multi engined aircraft. This leads to additional time being needed to establish the serviceability of such items. When duplication of certain equipment is required by regulations, e.g. 'the provision of a suction pump for each engine of a twin engined aircraft is a requirement under the British Civil Airworthiness Requirements', it should be understood that in this case it would be illegal to commence a flight if one of these pumps is found to be unserviceable.

In the case where two altimeters are fitted and one is found to be unserviceable prior to a VFR flight outside Controlled Airspace, it would not be illegal to continue the flight as planned. In this situation, however, the pilot must nevertheless bear in mind that operations in multi engined aircraft result in greater cockpit workloads and higher airspeeds than in a single engined aircraft. Because of this, an in-flight failure of the remaining altimeter could lead to the development of a situation involving greater hazard than may have seemed likely at first sight.

AIRCRAFT SERVICEABILITY
That the aircraft is in every way fit to fly . . .

The procedure for checking the aircraft documentation, e.g. Certificate of Airworthiness, Maintenance documents, etc., is the same as for single engined aircraft, but due to the added complexity and duplication of systems and instrumentation, the pre-flight inspection of the aircraft will be more involved and additional time will be required to complete this satisfactorily.

WEIGHT AND BALANCE
That the load carried is so distributed and secured . . .

This aspect of multi engined operation is usually more complex, and weight and balance calculations are required more often than in single engine aircraft. This is due to the greater weight carrying capacity and loading options with regard to passengers, fuel and baggage.

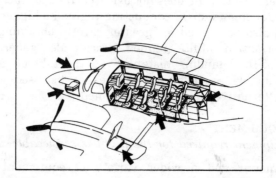

FUEL CALCULATIONS
That sufficient fuel and oil are carried and a safe margin allowed for contingencies . . .

The greater range and endurance capability, higher fuel consumption rates and additional fuel selection options of multi engined aircraft lead to the need for additional care to be taken when:

Calculating fuel requirements
Operating the fuel system
Using mixture control techniques.

It is not always appreciated by pilots that the greatest cause of engine failure is fuel exhaustion or starvation, either of which are attributable to a lack of pre-flight planning or improper fuel management procedures.

Further to this, *fuel contamination* is also a factor in some accidents and pilots must guard against this by supervising fuel uplifts and applying correct fuel strainer valve procedures.

AIRCRAFT PERFORMANCE
That due regard is given in respect of the aircraft performance . . .

An important consideration in this respect is that heavier aircraft require longer take-off and landing distances, and this must be allowed for in pre-flight preparation, not only in relation to the aerodromes of departure and destination, but also when planning for suitable alternatives.

Additionally, if one engine fails, the altitude capability of the aircraft is significantly affected, therefore in planning a route the single engine ceiling of the aircraft to be used must be taken into account.

An appreciation of the importance of this consideration can be illustrated by taking just one example of a modern high performance twin engined aeroplane and comparing the following figures from the aircraft manual:

SERVICE CEILING	
Both engines operating	19 750 feet
One engine operating	7400 feet

The example clearly illustrates the importance of this aspect during the planning stage of any navigation flight, particularly on those routes where mountainous terrain has to be overflown, and especially in many countries outside the United Kingdom.

The Air Navigation (General) Regulations

In addition to the operating conditions laid down in the Air Navigation Order and the Air Traffic Control Rules and Regulations, the private pilot who intends to obtain a multi engine Rating in his licence should in the interests of safety be fully aware of the reasons for the legislation in the Air Navigation (General) Regulations. Those specifically concerning the safety parameters involved in performance aspects of an aircraft under different conditions of aircraft weight, air temperature, wind conditions, etc., are particularly important. These are known as the Weight and Performance Regulations.

It should also be appreciated that the Airworthiness Division of the CAA is responsible for the approval and certification of aircraft placed upon the British Register. The document which details the requirements to meet this certification for small single and multi engined aircraft which do not exceed an all up weight of 5700 kg is the British Civil Airworthiness Requirements (BCARs) Section K.

WEIGHT AND PERFORMANCE

It is not intended that private pilots should have a detailed knowledge of the contents of either the Air Navigation (General) Regulations or the BCARs, but they should nevertheless understand the purpose of such documents. In particular, a pilot who wishes to obtain a multi engine Rating should understand the information contained in the following paragraphs concerning how and when these documents apply to the operation of multi engined aeroplanes.

Compliance with the airworthiness requirements and limitations is mandatory under the ANO, irrespective of the air navigation regulations applicable to the operations undertaken, e.g. Private, Public Transport, etc. Use of other information, such as the specific performance criteria laid down in the Air Navigation (General) Regulations, is only mandatory as and when prescribed by the air navigation regulations. Its use otherwise, although generally desirable on the grounds of safety, is at the discretion of the pilot in command of the aeroplane.

In other words, the Weight and Performance Regulations are not applicable to private flights, but their guidance should be followed whenever possible if the flight is to be conducted in accordance with the overall recommendations which are implicit in aircraft certification. To this end Weight and Performance is included in the AOPA Syllabus for the Multi Engine Rating, and a general review of performance factors is given on page 76 of this manual.

PERFORMANCE GROUPS

The BCARs detail minimum requirements for the approvals and certification required by the ANO, and for this purpose aeroplanes are divided into separate 'Performance Groups'. These Groups should not be confused with the 'Aircraft Groups' used in pilot licensing. The reason for separating aircraft into different Performance Groups is related to the need for regulations aimed at providing minimum acceptable levels of safety for fare paying passengers. Private flights do not come within the scope of these particular regulations, but regardless of this, they should whenever possible be used as a basis for any flight operation.

Those aircraft which do not exceed a maximum weight of 5700 kg are divided into Groups C, D and E. The table below outlines the differences between these three Groups.

PERFORMANCE GROUP

C	Aeroplanes with a performance level such that a forced landing should not be necessary if an engine fails *after take-off and initial climb.*
D	Aeroplanes with no specific provision for performance after engine failure.
E	Aeroplanes not exceeding 2730 kg, for which the extent of performance scheduling is limited. *Note:* Aeroplanes certificated in this performance Group will be capable of a performance level similar to that for Group C or Group D, but because of other factors or requirements involved in certification the manufacturer may prefer the aircraft to be placed in this performance Group, rather than C or D.

The performance of a particular aeroplane may be appropriate to one or more of the Performance Groups, but an individual aeroplane will only be classified for operation in one Performance Group.

This means that the owner or operator of a particular aircraft may apply for a specific aeroplane to be placed in any one of the Performance Groups which are applicable to its performance. This must be appreciated in order that the pilot understands that he may fly one particular make, type and model of aircraft which could be in a different Performance Group from an identical make, type and model which he has previously flown.

Therefore on those occasions when a pilot is required to abide by operating conditions applicable to the aircraft's particular Performance Group, or wishes to obtain the added safety which compliance with these regulations will provide, he should refer to the Certificate of Airworthiness or aircraft manual to determine in which Group the aeroplane is placed for certification purposes.

GENERAL PROVISIONS
The assessment of the ability of an aeroplane to comply with the Weight and Performance provisions of the Air Navigation (General) Regulations is detailed in Regulation 5. This Regulation specifies the relationship of the aircraft's Certification of Airworthiness and the Flight Manual or similar document, e.g. a Performance Schedule. It also includes certain definitions and directions used in the text of the Regulations for assessing the aircraft's Take-Off and Landing Weight, and the available distances which are declared at specific aerodromes. The relevant definitions are covered later in this manual in the section relating to Weight and Performance.

Regulations 8, 9 and 10 relate to aircraft which are certificated in Groups C, D and E respectively. As already mentioned these are applicable to Public Transport operations only, and do not legally apply to flights for private or training purposes. In summary, Regulations 8, 9 and 10 prescribe the minimum performance level for each phase of flight to enable the flight to be so planned, and the take-off weight adjusted, so that the required minimum performance is available.

It is necessary for pilots to be clear on the source of data to be used, since performance figures as well as aircraft handling requirements may be quoted in different types of publications. The Air Navigation Order refers the pilot first to the Certificate of Airworthiness, which may contain clauses bearing on performance and stating the source of any data, together with associated operating techniques. It is vital that flight planning is basd on the particular manual designated on the Certificate of Airworthiness.

The designated manual may be any one of the following:

- The UK Flight Manual.
- In the case of some imported aeroplanes, an English language Flight Manual approved by the Airworthiness Authority in the country of origin with a UK Supplement approved by the CAA.

  Note: The UK Supplement may include additional performance data which may supersede data in the main document.
- The Owner's Manual, or Pilot's Operating Handbook. These may also contain CAA approved supplements.

The reason why one aircraft may have an Owner's Manual or Pilot's Operating Handbook whereas another may have a Flight Manual relates largely to the aircraft certification procedures during the year of manufacture and the Category in which the particular aircraft is certificated.

The Flight Manual and Pilot's Operating Handbook contain information in greater detail than the Owner's Manual. Flight Manuals are normally required to be compiled and issued in respect of those aircraft operating in the Public Transport Category, and Owner's Manuals are now gradually being replaced by Pilot's Operating Handbooks.

METHODS OF FACTORING GROSS PERFORMANCE

Usually the Owner's Manual or Pilot's Operating Handbook will specify the length of the take-off run, and take-off distance, and landing run, and landing distance, applicable to the aircraft type.

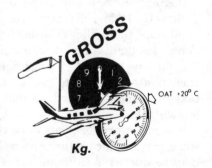

The figures are calculated for operating at maximum aircraft weight from a hard surface in zero wind conditions. These are shown in tables or graphs together with the modifications to allow for the direct effect of any differences in head-wind, ground surface, altitude, temperature and allowable aircraft weights.

When Public Transport operations are being conducted it is considered that certain safety factors must be integrated wth these data and therefore graphs which incorporate additional safety factors are normally incorporated in those Manuals approved by the CAA for aircraft engaged on Public Transport operations. This is known as *factoring* the original *gross performance figures* to make additional allowances in the interest of safety.

Most Flight Manuals therefore contain data in which these added factors have been included, while the Owner's Manuals or Pilot's Operating Handbooks normally contain only basic (gross) data.

The factored performance graphs take into account any small errors which might result from pilot technique or estimations, or slight inaccuracies in the information relating to aircraft weight, altitude, temperature and surface conditions.

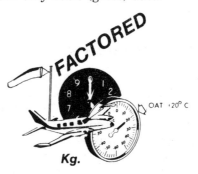

The wind factor which is used for these factored performance figures covers both tailwind and headwind conditions and in order to allow for variations in wind strength and direction only 50% of the headwind component is used. In the case of a tailwind situation the graph is factored to show 150% of the tailwind strength.

The take-off distances resulting from calculations made from these factored graphs are therefore a little longer than those originally shown in the manufacturer's manual or handbook for the specific aircraft type.

Flight planning considerations concerning the use of this performance information are covered on pages 79–84.

At this stage, Progress Test No 1 on page Q5 should be completed and the answers checked from the answer sheet on page Q36. As a result of this test the previous pages might need to be reviewed as necessary.

Flight on Asymmetric Power

THE PROBLEMS

The failure of one engine in a conventional twin engined aircraft will lead to a variety of different problems. These problems initially relate to an unbalance of the Thrust, Drag and Lift forces, all of which will affect a pilot's control over his aircraft. In addition to this the aircraft performance will be substantially reduced.

There will also be the human problems associated with the need to quickly recognise an engine failure, identify which engine has failed, and implement the procedures which have to be carried out. These procedures and the time available to implement them will vary with the flight situation in which the emergency takes place.

It will therefore be necessary for a pilot to understand the causes of these problems and to become competent at handling the various situations which may arise. He will also need to practise simulated engine failure at frequent intervals during conversion training and at regular intervals afterwards.

In all cases the pilot will have to maintain safe control of the aircraft and if an actual engine failure occurs he should in the interests of safety land at the nearest suitable aerodrome rather than continue with his planned flight.

Most problems which affect an aircraft in flight become more critical the closer the aircraft is to the ground and also when the airspeed is low. This is particularly so in the event of an engine failure occurring in a multi engined aeroplane. The amount of power being used at the time will also have a significant effect upon the pilot's ability to maintain control of the aircraft.

A large proportion of the time spent in flight training is to familiarise the pilot with, and teach him to become competent at, controlling the aircraft on one engine in the most critical conditions. These will inevitably be related to the take-off, circuit, approach and landing phases.

There are currently two distinct types of twin engined aircraft on the UK Register: the conventional twin with its engines disposed either side of the longitudinal axis, and the centre-line thrust variant which has its engines in line with the longitudinal axis.

CONTROL
&
PERFORMANCE

PERFORMANCE

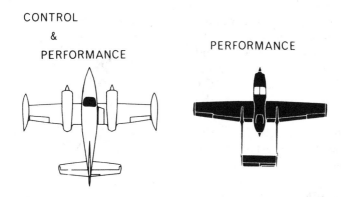

In the second case, if an engine failure occurs, there will be no asymmetry of Thrust, Drag or Lift, and the maintenance of control will be relatively straightforward; therefore the main problem with centre-line thrust aircraft concerns the substantially reduced performance.

ASYMMETRY

When an engine fails on a conventional twin engined aircraft the position of the engines relative to the aircraft's longitudinal axis will produce a degree of asymmetry of thrust and drag, and also, to a lesser extent, lift.

The unbalance of forces which result from these effects can be controlled provided sufficient airspeed is maintained. The yaw produced by the asymmetry of thrust and drag dictates that the most important primary control in this situation will be the rudder.

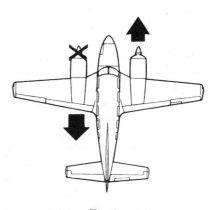

Fig 2

CONTROL

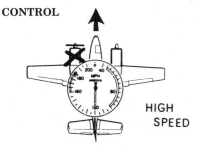

HIGH
SPEED

Twin engined aircraft are designed to ensure that the pilot can maintain control should one engine fail during flight. The degree of control available will however depend upon the aircraft's speed.

Below a certain minimum airspeed the degree of control will
be insufficient for directional and
lateral control to be maintained.
The airspeed will vary with the
power being developed by the
remaining engine, the amount of
drag, and the position of the
mean drag line relative to the
longitudinal axis.

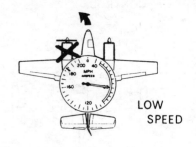

LOW
SPEED

PERFORMANCE

Although aircraft with more than one engine do normally have better
performance characteristics in relation to rate of climb, load carrying
capability, range, etc., there are two aspects of performance which are
particularly important when one engine fails. They are:

1. Take-off Run and Take-off Distance
2. Rate of Climb

In relation to 1 above, it can be said that although it is difficult to
make general comparisons between the take-off performance characteristics of the many single engined light aeroplanes relative to twin
engined light aeroplanes, certain basic figures can be considered. For
example, Table 1 gives the approximate Take-Off Run and Take-Off
Distances required by 4 representative light single engined aeroplanes. The figures are for International Standard Atmospheric
conditions at mean sea level and zero wind.

Representative Single Engined Aeroplanes

	Take-Off Run Feet	Take-Off Distance to 50' Feet
A	750	1400
B	850	1550
C	700	1350
D	1100	2000

Table 1

Examination of these figures shows that the Take-Off Run in each
case is about 50% of the distance required to clear a 50' obstacle.
However, when examining the respective Take-Off Run and Take-Off
Distances required by light multi engined aeroplanes it will be seen

that the Take-Off Run is approximately 75% of the Take-Off Distance. Table 2 shows the approximate Take-Off Run and Take-Off Distances required by 4 representative types of twin engined aeroplanes.

Representative Twin Engined Aeroplanes

	Take-Off Run Feet	Take-Off Distance to 50' Feet
A	1800	2400
B	1700	2300
C	1800	2300
D	1900	2450

Table 2

By referring to the Take-Off Run required by aircraft A in Table 1 (750') and comparing it with the Take-Off Run required by aircraft A in Table 2 (1800') it will be seen that another significant fact emerges, which is that a light twin engined aircraft might require a Take-Off Run of at least 1000' more than a single engined type.

There are various reasons for this difference in performance between light single engined aeroplanes and light twin engined aeroplanes, not the least important of these being the additional weight of a twin engined aircraft and the increased *distance* needed to accelerate to the *higher* speed required for lift off.

A further comparison is in the distance needed to stop the aircraft should a serious fault develop during the take-off run.

In the case of the light single engined aircraft suffering, for example, an engine failure just before lift off, there will usually be ample room to slow down and stop when using normal aerodromes. However, in the case of the light twin engined aircraft with its higher lift off speed and greater weight and therefore greater inertia, an engine failure in the same circumstances can result in situations where this distance might be marginal, or even totally inadequate.

THE FORCES AND COUPLES

An aircraft which is being flown correctly in laterally level flight, at a constant altitude, a constant airspeed and on a constant heading, will be in equilibrium and in balanced flight. This means that the forces of

Lift and Weight are equal, the forces of Thrust and Drag are equal and the aircraft is in a state of balance, i.e. no yaw or sideslip will be present.

In Fig 3 it will be seen that the net result of the couples produced by (a) Lift and Weight and (b) Thrust and Drag will lead to the need for a downward force on the tailplane to balance the nose down effect of the two couples.

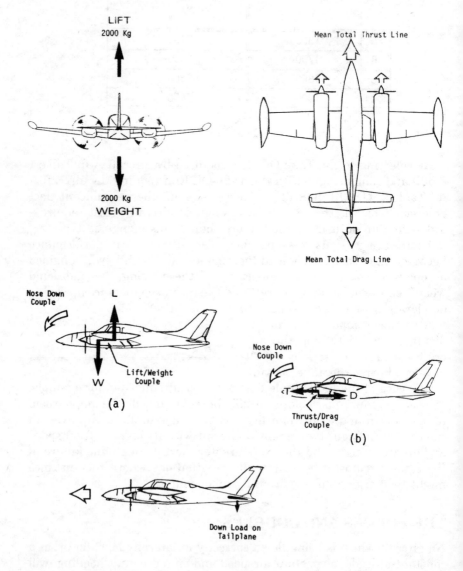

Fig 3

SYMMETRY

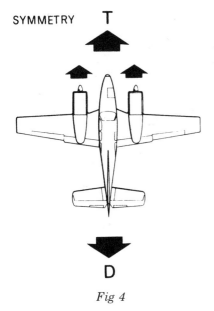

Fig 4

In plan view, the Thrust and Drag forces will be in equal proportion and aligned with each other, so that no asymmetry of thrust or drag will be present (see Fig 4).

OFFSET THRUST LINE

In the case of a conventional twin engined aircraft with its engines mounted on the wings it can be seen that when both engines are operating at the same power, the thrust force from each engine will be symmetrical, but the failure of one engine will alter this balance and create the thrust situation illustrated in Fig 5.

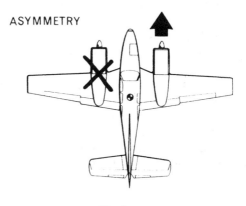

Fig 5

The result of this asymmetrical thrust will cause a yawing moment towards the failed engine (Fig 6(a)). This yawing moment at any given airspeed will be greatest when the operating engine is producing maximum power and the other engine is developing zero power (Fig 6(b)). The strength of the yawing moment will also be affected by the position of the engine in relation to the aircraft's longitudinal axis, i.e. the further out an engine is placed on the aircraft wing, the stronger the yawing moment will become. Therefore aircraft designers try to place the engines as close to the fuselage as other design requirements will permit.

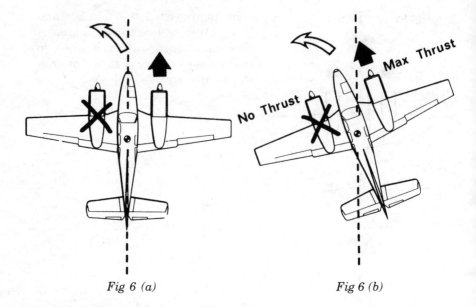

Fig 6 (a)   Fig 6 (b)

ASYMMETRIC BLADE EFFECT

In addition to the asymmetric power effect due to the location of the engines on the aircraft wing, a small component of asymmetric propeller thrust will be present during single engined flight. This has a small but significant effect during single engined flight at low airspeeds.

Asymmetric blade effect occurs because reduced power leads to a lower airspeed and therefore an aircraft will have to be flown at a slightly higher angle of attack in order to provide the required lift. This will result in the descending propeller blade having a higher angle of attack than the ascending blade. The descending blade will therefore produce more thrust. This is illustrated diagrammatically in Fig 7.

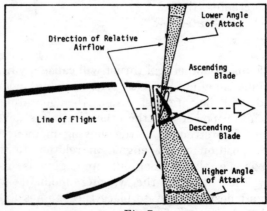

Fig 7

Added to this is the fact that the greater the aircraft's angle of attack the greater is the difference in the speed between the upgoing and downgoing blades of the propeller relative to the air.

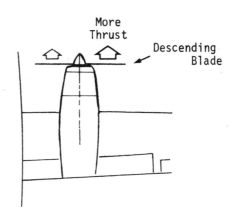

Figure 8 illustrates this effect and it can be seen that during the time that the aircraft moves from A to B, the downgoing blade will travel a greater distance than the upgoing blade, therefore the downgoing blade will be travelling faster and producing more thrust.

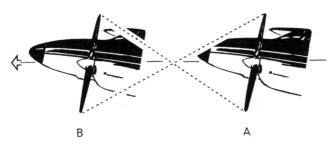

B   A

Fig 8

These two effects combine to create a thrust line which is slightly offset from the engine centre line. The side to which it is offset will depend upon the direction of rotation of the propeller, but in most of the modern light twins the propeller rotates in a clockwise direction (as viewed from behind) so the actual thrust line will usually be offset to the right.

In Fig 9 the disposition of the thrust forces are representative of an aircraft with propellers which rotate clockwise, and it will be seen that failure of the left engine will mean that a larger yawing moment will be created, because the thrust of the right engine is further out from the longitudinal axis of the aircraft.

The term *Critical Engine* is used to describe the engine which, if failed, will lead to the largest yawing moment for any given set of conditions. The critical engine in the aircraft shown in Fig 9 is the left engine. Additional factors which determine the strength of asymmetric yaw will be the amount of engine torque and the slipstream angle from the operating engine relative to the vertical tail surface.

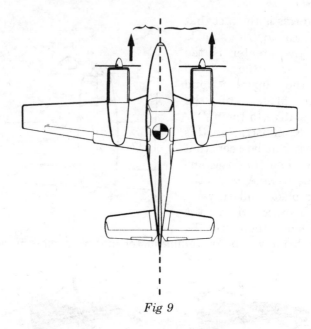

Fig 9

Sometimes an aircraft manufacturer will arrange the propellers to rotate in opposite directions, in which case the yaw produced in asymmetric flight will have the same magnitude regardless of which engine fails, and there will be no critical engine.

OFFSET DRAG LINE – FAILED ENGINE DRAG AND TOTAL DRAG INCREASE

Apart from the additional induced drag resulting from the need to increase the angle of attack to maintain constant altitude, there will also be a positive increase in the drag produced by the propeller of the failed engine which is being windmilled by the airflow. This windmilling effect causes a considerable increase in drag, which will add to the yawing effect produced by the operating engine. Therefore the disposition of the couples affecting the directional control of the aircraft during single engined flight will be as shown in Fig 10.

It can therefore be seen that during asymmetric flight there will be an increase in total drag, and the strength of the Thrust-Drag couple will depend upon the thrust being developed from the operating engine and the asymmetric drag produced by the windmilling propeller.

ASYMMETRY OF LIFT – PROPELLER SLIPSTREAM EFFECT

Whilst the initial yaw produced by the asymmetric thrust and drag takes place, inertia will for a short time cause the aircraft to continue along its original line of flight. During this period the effect of yaw

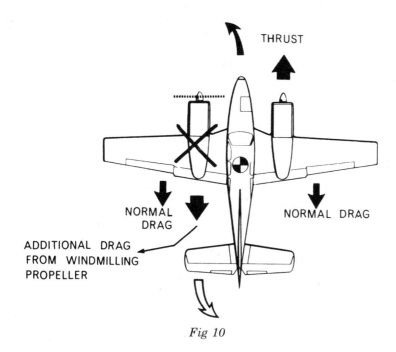

Fig 10

will cause the outer wing to travel slightly faster than the inner wing and produce more lift. This, together with the effects of dihedral, will result in a rolling action towards the inoperative engine.

In addition to this, whenever asymmetric power conditions exist, a rolling effect will occur due to the loss of slipstream behind the failed engine. This loss of slipstream causes a small but significant loss of lift from the wing area behind the propeller of the failed engine and therefore a condition of unequal lift between the two wings will result. This also leads to a rolling action in the direction of the failed engine (see Fig 11).

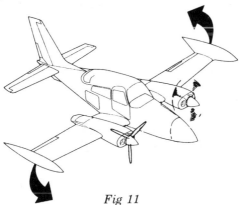

Fig 11

Further to this, and as a result of the asymmetric yawing moment, an additional loss of airflow will occur over the wing on the same side as the failed engine. This is due to the blanking effect of the fuselage which results from the aircraft yawing. Figure 12 illustrates this effect.

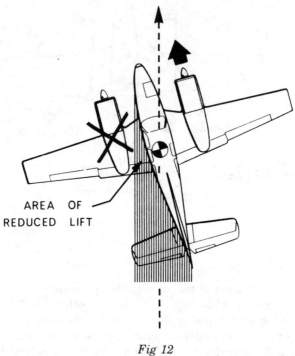

AREA   OF
REDUCED   LIFT

Fig 12

To summarise, if no corrective action is taken to control the aircraft following an engine failure, the aircraft will yaw and roll into the direction of the inoperative engine, and the cumulative effects of reduced power, additional drag, and the reduction of airspeed and lift will result in a loss of altitude unless some corrective measures are taken.

SIDE FORCES

The yawing moment created by the asymmetric thrust and drag can be counteracted by the use of rudder, but after this has been done a condition will exist where the aircraft is flown at a slight angle to the relative airflow, and therefore a small amount of sideways slip towards the inoperative engine will occur.

In this situation the side force produced by the fuselage and the small side force created by the thrust line being at a slight angle to the line of flight will be balanced by the side force produced from the rudder (Fig 13). At normal cruising airspeeds or above, this angle to

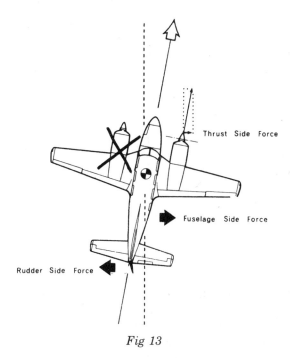

Thrust Side Force

Fuselage Side Force

Rudder Side Force

Fig 13

the relative airflow will be relatively small, and amount to only a few degrees.

Although this configuration will produce a net side force of zero, because the rudder and fuselage and thrust side forces balance out, the angle at which the aircraft is now presented to the airflow creates additional drag. At normal airspeeds the wings can however still be held level and the ball of the balance indicator kept in the centre.

EFFECT OF BANK

When an engine fails at low airspeed, the effectiveness of the rudder in counteracting yaw is reduced, but directional control can be assisted by banking the aircraft towards the operating engine. It should nevertheless be appreciated that care must be used in relation to the amount of bank applied.

This is because when bank is used the amount of lift directly opposing weight will be reduced (the lift line being tilted to one side, Fig 14) and therefore either the angle of attack, or the airspeed, or both, will need to be increased to replace the 'lost lift'. These measures will also create more drag and a further increase in thrust will be demanded. Extra thrust may not be available, and in any case increased thrust will worsen the degree of asymmetry.

Further to this, when bank is used the balance indicator will show a condition of sideslip and the pilot will not therefore be able to

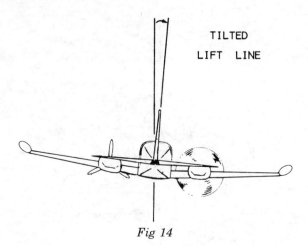

TILTED
LIFT LINE

Fig 14

estimate the degree of balance being achieved, and little or no
warning of an approaching critical control condition may exist.
Therefore on those occasions when bank is required to assist
directional control it should be limited to a small amount.

At higher airspeeds the rudder alone will be effective enough to
counteract the yaw forces produced from asymmetric thrust and drag,
and a condition where the aircraft's longitudinal axis is more closely
aligned with the aircraft's flight path will occur (Fig 15).

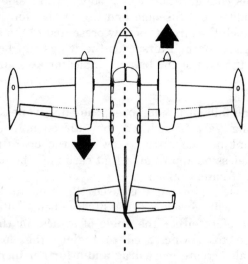

Fig 15

EFFECT AND CONTROL OF YAW IN STRAIGHT AND TURNING FLIGHT

During straight flight and provided sufficient airspeed is maintained, the yaw set up by the asymmetric thrust and drag following engine failure can be recognised and corrected by the use of rudder. The wings can also be kept in a laterally level condition and the balance indicator centred.

During turning flight however, two important factors will be the airspeed and the direction of turn relative to the failed engine. For example, if the left engine has failed the aircraft will want to yaw, roll and turn to the left, and therefore to initiate and maintain a left turn will present little difficulty. It will only be necessary to reduce the amount of right rudder being used to counteract the left yaw, and to control the bank angle with ailerons. However, in the same situation a balanced right turn will require additional right rudder. At low speeds the amount of right rudder needed will be large, and it may therefore be necessary to limit the turn to small angles of bank if balance is to be maintained.

This latter point is important during turns onto base leg, and final approach, when a circuit is being flown, and the direction of the traffic pattern requires turns to be made towards the operating engine.

Recognition of engine failure during climbing or level turns is straightforward, as the aircraft will yaw towards the failed engine, and provided the airspeed is close to or above the normal cruising speed, no control difficulties should occur. In these conditions sufficient rudder and aileron control will be available to either return the aircraft to straight flight, or maintain the turn.

At any time when low power is being used and the airspeed is relatively high, e.g. in the descent phase, it will be more difficult to recognise an engine failure as the yaw and roll forces will be very small. This will be the case whether a straight or turning descent is being executed at the time.

THRUST AND RUDDER SIDE FORCE COUPLES – MOMENT ARMS

The effect of side forces, their couples and moment arms have been broadly covered under a previous heading, 'Side Forces'. However, it will be of value to repeat that when the initial yaw occurs following an engine failure, the application of rudder to counteract this yaw will produce a side force.

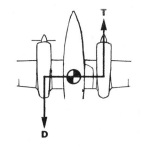

The immediate situation is one where the rudder side force and thrust and drag forces are unbalanced. The pilot will appreciate this is taking place as it will be indicated by the ball of the balance indicator.

A further increase in rudder application will then position the ball in the centre. Once the yaw is neutralised by sufficient application of rudder and the wings held level, the ball will be central but the aircraft will be flying at a slight angle to the relative airflow. Although it should be noted that at normal cruising speeds this angle is very small, it will nevertheless result in a significant increase in drag.

Control in Asymmetric Power Flight

Clearly, when one engine fails the most important consideration in controlling the aircraft is airspeed. At cruising or higher airspeeds there will be little difficulty in controlling the effects of yaw and roll. Plenty of time will also be available to ascertain the cause, remedy it where possible, or carry out the required drills to shut down the failed engine and set the aircraft up for continued flight on one engine.

However, if an engine fails when the airspeed is low, the situation is more critical and it will immediately require correct and positive responses from the pilot to maintain a safe flight condition.

USE, MISUSE, AND LIMITS OF RUDDER, AILERONS AND ELEVATORS

The effectiveness of all flying controls is related to the amount of their deflection, and to the indicated airspeed at the particular time. The lower the IAS, the greater the control deflection necessary to obtain a given effect.

Although yaw is initiated and prevented primarily by the rudder, it must be appreciated that the elevators also play a vital part in maintaining adequate control, because assuming a fixed power setting, it is the elevators which will control the airspeed, and therefore their use will influence the effectiveness of both the rudder and ailerons.

Provided altitude and power are sufficient, a safe airspeed can be maintained, which permits the rudder and aileron to be used without excessive deflection. Nevertheless, because a combination of rudder and aileron is used to prevent yaw and roll, the pilot must take care to avoid a situation where control is maintained by insufficient rudder and too much aileron. The correct procedure is to use the rudder to control yaw, together with a minimum amount of aileron deflection to keep the wings level.

EFFECT OF BANK AND SIDESLIP, BALANCE – FIN STALL POSSIBILITY

If, when an engine fails, the ailerons alone are used to hold the aircraft on a steady heading, a large angle of sideslip would occur, and the pilot would be unable to use the balance indicator to give an immediate warning of imminent control difficulties. Also, at large sideslip angles, the fin may stall, leading to a rapid deterioration in control. Additionally the resulting large horizontal aerodynamic force acting on the fin, prior to it stalling, may be such that the structural limitations of this component may be exceeded.

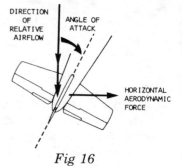

Fig 16

DECREASE OF THE AVAILABLE EFFECTIVE DISPLACEMENT OF AILERON AND RUDDER

For a given set of circumstances, when the critical engine has failed, a larger rudder deflection will be needed to combat the additional yaw. In effect this will mean that the remaining effective displacement of the rudder will be less when the critical engine has failed, particularly during those manoeuvres when turns are being made towards the operating engine. Similarly for the ailerons; thus if full aileron movement is required to recover from a turbulence induced upset it will not be available because some deflection is already being used to overcome the asymmetric effects.

During a turn made towards the operating engine there may also be a tendency for the pilot to attempt to increase the rate of turn by additional use of ailerons. This can lead to a condition of marked unbalance, and a positive further deterioration in aircraft performance because of the additional drag from both the fuselage and the ailerons.

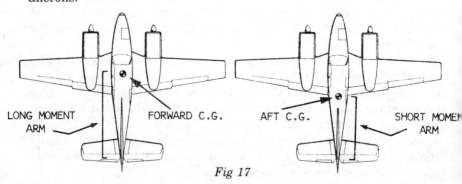

Fig 17

The position of the centre of gravity will also affect the available displacement of the controls for any given set of conditions. This occurs because the aircraft yaws about its centre of gravity, and the further aft the centre of gravity, the shorter will be the rudder moment arm. This therefore reduces its effective displacement in terms of yaw control (see Fig 17).

EFFECT OF IAS AND THRUST – EFFECTIVENESS OF FLYING CONTROLS

The lower the airspeed the less will be the available effectiveness of the flying controls. Therefore the most critical control situation will occur at low airspeed and with maximum thrust being produced from the operating engine.

EFFECT OF RESIDUAL UNBALANCED FORCES – FOOT LOAD AND TRIMMING

The FAA certification requirements for twin engined aircraft up to a weight of 5700 kg call for the following maximum rudder control forces being applied by the pilot experiencing an engine failure.

FORCE AS APPLIED TO RUDDER PEDALS	lbs Force
Temporary Application	150
Prolonged Application	20

Use of the rudder trim controls can be considered in two distinct situations:

As an aid to obtaining sufficient rudder deflection if the pilot has insufficient strength to prevent yaw occurring.
As an aid to reducing fatigue once the pilot has corrected for the asymmetric flight condition.

In the first case it should be appreciated that if it is possible to reduce power on the operating engine, this will immediately reduce the amount of yaw being experienced. In the second case it will clearly be an important benefit to accurately trim out the rudder force in order to reduce pilot fatigue and workload during continued flight on one engine.

Minimum Control and Safety Speeds

If an engine fails when the aircraft is being flown below a certain minimum indicated airspeed the pilot will be unable to maintain directional control. This minimum speed will vary with many factors, e.g. the power being used on the operating engine, the amount of asymmetric drag, etc.

DEFINITION, DERIVATION AND FACTORS AFFECTING V_{mc} (MINIMUM CONTROL SPEED)

In order to establish a minimum speed at which the pilot could maintain control in the event of one engine failing on a particular aircraft, the aircraft certification procedures use the term V_{mc} (Minimum Control Speed), which is defined as follows:

- V_{mc} is the lowest airspeed at which, when any engine is suddenly made inoperative, it is still possible to recover control of the aeroplane with that engine inoperative and to maintain straight flight, either with zero yaw, or, at the option of the pilot, with an angle of bank of not more than 5° (see note). This airspeed shall be such that during recovery, the aeroplane must not assume any dangerous attitude nor should the pilot require exceptional piloting skill, alertness or strength, to prevent a change in heading of more than 20°.
- It must be understood that V_{mc} is related only to control of the aeroplane, and is not related to aircraft performance, e.g. climb capability. The certification requirements for small twin engined aircraft do not demand that the aircraft be capable of climbing either at V_{mc}, or at a higher airspeed.
- The V_{mc} (indicated airspeed) published in the Flight/Owner's Manual/Pilot's Operating Handbook is normally established for the take-off condition using the following criteria and in these circumstances it is known as V_{mca} (Minimum Control Speed Air):
    1. Full take-off power on the operating engine.
    2. The rearmost allowable centre of gravity.

3. Flaps in the take-off position.
4. The landing gear retracted.
5. The propeller of the inoperative engine windmilling in the fine pitch position (rpm level fully forward).

● V_{mca} is a certification speed intended to be the basis for determining the operating procedures concerned primarily with controllability, and only indirectly with performance. It is not expected that the average pilot will normally be able to control the aeroplane safely at V_{mca}, especially in critical or adverse circumstances near the ground at this speed, and particularly in the conditions described in 1 to 5 above. (BCARs Section K, chapter 2–8 refers.) The figure is obtained by applying a special technique very cautiously, one which does not provide for the element of surprise. It is a dynamic flight condition only, and one where a small handling error could lead to serious consequences.

Note: It should be noted that in a number of multi engined aircraft the application of 5 degrees of bank towards the operating engine can significantly reduce the V_{mc}. It is therefore quite common for manufacturers to use a 5 degree bank angle during certification trials in order to quote the lowest V_{mc} for their product.

All pilots who operate multi engined aircraft must know the V_{mca} for each type they fly and appreciate that controlled flight below this speed is impossible unless the conditions at which it applies are changed, e.g. the power is reduced on the operating engine, or the asymmetric drag is reduced.

Therefore if an aircraft is allowed to become airborne before reaching V_{mca}, and an engine fails at this stage, the pilot will have to reduce power immediately and lower the aircraft nose in order to maintain control. This will normally mean that an immediate landing is unavoidable.

The various factors which affect the minimum speed at which control of the aircraft can be maintained in event of the failure of one engine, are listed below:

Power of the operating engine
Aircraft weight and the position of the centre of gravity
Altitude
Position of the landing gear, wing flaps and engine cowl flaps
Total drag and position of the drag line
Propeller drag and effect of feathering
Whether the failed engine is the critical engine
Amount of bank applied towards the operating engine
Turbulence and wind gusts
Pilot reaction and strength

EFFECT OF POWER

The force producing the yaw is proportional to the thrust from the operating engine. Therefore at a given IAS more rudder will be required to maintain directional control if the thrust is increased. The greater the thrust from the operating engine, the higher will be the IAS at which directional control is lost.

EFFECT OF WEIGHT AND CENTRE OF GRAVITY POSITION

The greater the all up weight of the aircraft, the greater the angle of attack for a given airspeed. Increased weight also reduces the rate of acceleration. Therefore an increase in weight will create an increase in induced drag and a reduced rate of acceleration, both of which are important factors when operating close to the V_{mc}.

The effect of the position of the centre of gravity has already been covered but can be summarised here as, the further aft the centre of gravity becomes, the smaller will be the rudder moment arm, and therefore the greater the deflection required from the rudder to maintain directional control for a given airspeed.

EFFECT OF ALTITUDE

In the case of normally aspirated engines the thrust obtainable from the operating engine will decrease with a gain in altitude and as a result the V_{mc} in terms of indicated airspeed will decrease as altitude is gained. This is because the maximum power available from the engine decreases with the lessening air density which occurs during the climb. When the aircraft is equipped with supercharged or turbocharged engines, the sea level thrust will however be maintained up to higher altitudes during which, at full power on the operating engine, the indicated V_{mc} will remain unchanged.

With increase of altitude the TAS at which the aircraft will stall will increase, but the IAS at the stall will be the same for all altitudes. With non supercharged or non turbocharged engines, however, the V_{mc} (IAS) will become less as altitude is gained.

Therefore in the case of an aircraft which has a V_{mc} above

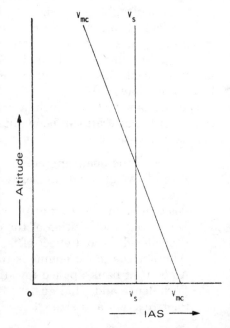

the stalling speed at sea level, at altitude a situation could occur where the stalling speed (IAS) is greater than the V_{mc}.

EFFECT OF LANDING GEAR, WING FLAPS AND COWL FLAPS
The effect on V_{mc} of these systems relates to the additional drag effect in respect of the asymmetric drag line. Anything which increases the strength of the drag/thrust couple will lead to an increase in the V_{mc}.

Additionally, and depending upon the type of landing gear fitted, i.e. folding forward or rearward instead of sideways during lowering or raising, the centre of gravity may be slightly changed during landing gear operation. Any movement of the landing gear which leads to a rearward movement of the centre of gravity will increase the V_{mc}.

The effect from the drag resulting from the cowl flaps or cooling gills being open will be significant, and they should be closed on the inoperative engine as soon as possible.

Note: Depending upon the aerodynamic design of the intake entry and the disposition of the cowl flaps or cooling gills, it may be that the minimum drag position occurs at that point just before they are completely closed, and this should be determined for the particular aircraft type by visual inspection.

Figure 18 shows two types of cowl flap design which illustrate the differences which may be found between cooling systems in current use.

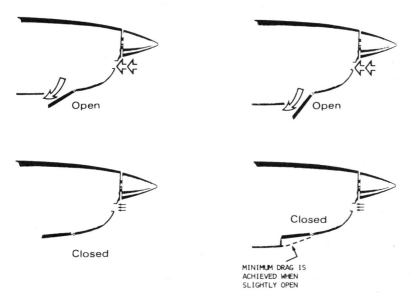

Fig 18

EFFECT OF DRAG

If an engine fails when the aircraft is close to the V_{mca} it is vital to minimise the effect of drag as soon as possible. The effects of landing gear, flaps, and cowl flaps or cooling gills have already been covered in relation to total drag and the offset drag line. It should also be borne in mind that when operating in aircraft where landing lights are used as an operational procedure during take-off and landing, and such lights are of the retractable type, their effect upon drag can be significant at flight near V_{mc}, and they should therefore be retracted as quickly as possible.

Another factor in relation to total drag is the amount incurred by the flaps relative to the landing gear, and this could have a bearing upon which of these two should be initially selected to the up position.

If a large amount of flap is being used at the stage where an engine fails and the airspeed is close to V_{mca}, it is quite likely that drag will be minimised more quickly by selecting flaps to the take-off position immediately and prior to selecting the landing gear to the up position. Such a situation would normally only arise if engine failure occurred when an aircraft was near the ground, e.g. when carrying out a missed approach from a very low height or going round again following a normal landing.

Advice on the correct retraction sequence will normally be given in the 'Emergency Section' of the aircraft manual and this usually takes into account the effect of the landing gear movement upon the centre of gravity position, and the effect of the wing flaps upon the pitching moment of the aircraft, e.g. downwash effect over the tailplane, changes in the lift/weight couple and aerodynamic pitching moments, etc., and it will normally be advisable to follow the sequence listed in the Flight/Owner's Manual or Pilot's Operating Handbook for type.

PROPELLER DRAG – EFFECT OF FEATHERING

The windmilling propeller of the failed engine will produce a large amount of asymmetric drag. The effect of this drag will be most critical at the lower airspeeds experienced during the take-off period. If the propeller is feathered, this drag will be significantly reduced, and therefore as soon as practical following an engine failure the feathering procedure should be carried out.

EFFECT OF THE CRITICAL ENGINE FAILING

When the propeller rotation is in the same direction for both engines, the slipstream and asymmetric blade effects will cause one engine to have a higher minimum control speed than the other. In engines which rotate clockwise (as viewed from behind) failure of the left engine will result in a higher V_{mc}. This is taken into account when establishing V_{mca} for the particular aircraft.

AMOUNT OF BANK APPLIED TOWARDS THE OPERATING ENGINE

If an engine fails when the aircraft is being flown at normal climbing speed or more, it is usual for the pilot to fly the aircraft with the wings level and in a balanced condition. However, flight tests have shown that if the airspeed is low (say between V_{mca} and V_{yse}) a significant advantage will be gained by banking up to 5 degrees towards the operating engine. This action will reduce the $V_{mc,}$ reduce the sideslip effect and improve the rate of climb on one engine.

EFFECT OF TURBULENCE AND WIND GUSTS

When turbulent and gusty weather conditions exist this will affect the ability of the pilot to maintain directional control. This is due to the fact that during flight at V_{mc} the rudder will be fully deflected, thus leaving no margin for any corrections in yaw which may be necessitated by air turbulence. Therefore during turbulent and gusty weather conditions it will be particularly important to avoid flying at airspeeds close to V_{mc}.

EFFECT OF PILOT REACTION AND STRENGTH

Clearly, the faster the pilot's reaction to a sudden failure of one engine, the more easily and quickly he will obtain control over the aircraft. However the physical strength and skill of the pilot will also be important factors in a critical situation, such as flight at, or close to, the minimum control speed.

It is for this reason that it is extremely important for a pilot to adjust his seat during the flight preparation stage, to ensure that he is fully capable of obtaining full rudder travel. Skill developed from practice will also be important, in that a skilful pilot will be able more easily to handle the additional workload brought about by sudden engine failure.

DEFINITION, DERIVATION OF V_2 (TAKE-OFF SAFETY SPEED)

Because V_{mc} is the minimum speed at which directional control can be maintained, it would be advisable for considerations of safety to reach a slightly higher speed than this during the take-off run and before lift off.

For example, a engine failure occurring above V_{mc} will give the pilot greater control whilst conducting the necessary engine failure procedures. For this reason a Take-Off Safety Speed (V_2) is defined in the regulations and interpreted in the following paragraph.

A minimum speed used during the take-off phase, at which, if failure of the critical engine occurs, a safe margin above V_{mca} exists, which should enable the pilot to maintain satisfactory control of the aircraft. The selected speed should be the greater of either 1·1 times the V_{mca}, or 1·2 times the stalling speed in the take-off configuration.

Take-Off Safety Speed (V_2), which may vary according to the aircraft's configuration and other factors, therefore contains elements concerned with controllability (and with performance) of light twin engined aircraft, and is expressed as an indicated airspeed. It is in any case a factored V_{mca}, or a factored stalling speed on which to base a decision whether to abandon take-off, re-land or force land, or attempt to accelerate to the best single engine climb speed if the prevailing conditions permit, and provided all unnecessary drag has been removed.

Thus it will be seen that in normal flying operations there is a need for a surplus of speed above V_{mca} to allow for the element of surprise and other factors in the prevailing circumstances which govern the actual airspeed at which any particular pilot would be able to control a particular aircraft should an engine fail suddenly during the take-off phase.

Once determined, the speed can be used as a *Decision Speed* to establish whether to abandon the take-off, or if already airborne, to re-land, force land, or continue the flight and accelerate to single engined climbing speed.

Note: In high performance aircraft such as airliners, 'Decision Speed' is achieved during the take-off run whilst the aircraft is on the ground, and is known as V_1. This V definition is not applicable to light twin engined aircraft which are certificated in Performance Groups C, D or E, but only to those aeroplanes certificated in Performance Group A.

↓↓   **NORMAL TAKEOFF DISTANCE**

Weight lbs	Take-Off To 50' Obstacle Speed KIAS	Pressure Altitude Feet	-10 C (14 F)		0 C (32 F)		10 C (50 F)	
			Ground Roll Feet	Total Distance To Clear 50'	Ground Roll Feet	Total Distance To Clear 50'	Ground Roll Feet	Total Distance To Clear 50'
5100	88	Sea Level	1320	2200	1450	2310	1560	2420
		1000	1460	2360	1590	2490	1710	2640
		2000	1600	2540	1750	2690	1890	2870
		3000	1770	2750	1930	2910	2080	3200
		4000	1950	2980	2140	3170	2380	3520
		5000	2180	3250	2440	3530	2630	3870

Fig 19

In the case of the small multi engined aircraft being discussed in this manual it should be understood that the term V_2 is not used in relation to American certification requirements of light twin engined aircraft and this sometimes leads to confusion when American manufactured light aircraft are being used in the UK (V_2 may however be found in the UK Supplement to the Flight Manual). Secondly it must also be appreciated that some multi engined aircraft cannot achieve a Safety Speed within the strict definition of V_2 whilst on the ground because of control problems, i.e. 'wheelbarrowing'. In this case V_2 may be considered as the speed to achieve on reaching 50' above the ground (refer to page 67). This is because the aircraft certification procedures require a particular speed to be quoted (higher than V_{mca}) and used to calculate the take-off distance to 50' above the ground (refer to Fig 19).

Therefore when V_2 is not quoted, the 50' speed as shown in the performance tables or graphs of the specific aircraft manual could be used. In the case of those aircraft which are controllable up to V_2 whilst on the ground, the terms Safety Speed, Recommended Safe Single Engine Speed or Decision Speed will normally be quoted in the aircraft manual (refer to Fig 20). In the unusual circumstances of neither figure being available, the CAA Airworthiness Division should be asked for guidance.

SINGLE-ENGINE AIRSPEEDS FOR SAFE OPERATION

Conditions:
1. Take-Off Weight   5100 lbs.
2. Landing Weight   5000 lbs.
3 Standard Day, Sea Level.

Air Mininum Control Speed	80 KIAS
Recommended Safe Single Engine Speed	88 KIAS
Best Single Engine Angle of Climb Speed	96 KIAS
Best Single Engine Rate of Climb Speed (Flaps Up) ...	101 KIAS

Fig 20

OTHER V CODES

V_{sse}

Many twin engined aircraft have a stalling speed which is close to (either above or below) the V_{mca}. This could lead to a dangerous situation if an engine failure was simulated when the aircraft was operating at high power and close to the V_{mca}, where an uncontrollable yaw leading to a spin might easily result.

To avoid this possibility a new term, V_{sse}, has recently been defined by the Federal Aviation Administration for American manufactured multi engined aircraft. This airspeed is for the guidance of pilots practising engine failure. The definition of V_{sse} is as follows:

V_{sse} | The recommended safe one engine inoperative speed which provides a safe margin above V_{mca}, to ensure the availability of control, and to guard against the possibility of entering a spin when one engine is suddenly stopped.

Sudden simulated engine failure below V_{sse} is now being prohibited by the manufacturers of currently built American twin engined aircraft. When V_{sse} is not quoted in the Flight Manual or equivalent document (as will be the case in earlier manufactured aircraft), the pilot practising single engine procedures should ensure that simulated sudden engine failures are not made at a speed less than about 10 knots above V_{mca} or less than V_2 for the aircraft type.

V_y AND V_{yse}

This is the speed which will give the maximum rate of climb with all engines operating. Obviously this speed will change when one engine is inoperative, and it will normally be lower. The single engined best rate of climb speed is termed V_{yse}.

V_x AND V_{xse}

This is the best angle of climb speed, and will give the greatest altitude for a given distance of forward travel. This speed will also change when one engine is inoperative and will normally be lower. The single engined best angle of climb speed is termed V_{xse}.

Note: Another term which is often used in relation to minimum control speed in asymmetric flight is *Critical Speed*. However, as this expression is not defined in any official civil publication, different interpretations of its meaning are given in different books and training notes. Therefore the term is not used in this manual.

Enter the V code airspeeds for your training aircraft in the appropriate spaces on Table 3.

V SPEEDS		YOUR A/C
Minimum Control (Single Engine)	V_{MC}	
Take-Off Safety Speed	V_2	
Best Angle-of-Climb (Flaps Up)	V_X	
Best Angle-of-Climb (Single Engine)	V_{XSE}	
Best Rate of Climb (Flaps Up)	V_Y	
Best Rate of Climb (Single Engine)	V_{YSE}	
Maximum Landing Gear Operating	V_{LO}	
Maximum Landing Gear Extended	V_{LE}	
Maximum Flap Extended (Full)	V_{FE}	
Maximum Flap Extended (First Increment)		
Maneuvering	V_A	
Maximum Structural Cruising	V_{NO}	
Never Exceed	V_{NE}	
* Recommended Safe Single Engine	V_{sse}	
Stall (Gear and Flaps Down)	V_{so}	

Table 3
*This speed is an operational safety speed for training purposes

Effects on Performance of One Engine Inoperative

In relation to the performance characteristics of a twin engined aeroplane it is extremely important to appreciate that although at first sight it would appear that two engines automatically give a higher safety factor, the margin can in certain flight situations be a very small one.

In the case of a single engined aircraft the pilot quite clearly knows that in the event of engine failure there is only one direction the aircraft can go, i.e. downwards. In this case, the pilot's primary action is to maintain sufficient airspeed and search for the most suitable landing area. In the case of one engine failing on a twin engined aircraft, the course of action will not be as simple as this, and the following paragraphs explain why.

A common misconception in relation to a twin engined aircraft which suffers an engine failure is that only half the available performance will be lost, whereas in fact it is half the *total engine power* which has been lost. To some this statement may seem to be splitting hairs, but it must be appreciated that there is a significant difference between *power* and *performance*. To understand this more clearly, it will be useful to review the basic power curves as they relate to an aeroplane.

Performance can be rated for different considerations such as speed, rate of climb, rate of descent (in the gliding situation), range, load carrying capability, etc. In the case of multi engined aircraft which suffer an engine failure, the most important of these will be the *rate of climb*.

Referring to Fig 21 it can be seen that V_y (the best rate of climb speed) is that airspeed where the largest amount of thrust horsepower is available beyond that required for level flight. This is known as the *excess thrust horsepower*.

EFFECT ON POWER CURVES

Assuming each engine supplies 150 hp, the failure of one will leave only 150 hp available. Plotting this across the diagram in Fig 22 will

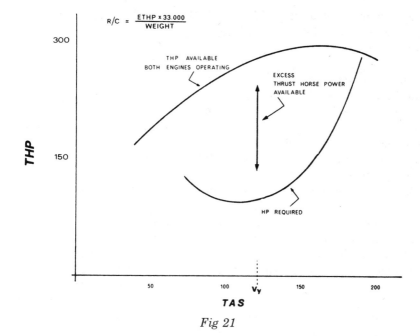

Fig 21

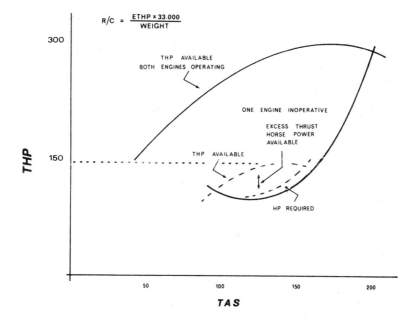

Fig 22

clearly show a drastic reduction in the excess thrust horsepower which is available for climbing purposes.

POWER AVAILABLE FOR CLIMBING AND MANOEUVRING

In the circumstances shown in Fig 22, the aircraft will be capable of maintaining level flight, but due to the small amount of excess thrust horsepower available, the rate of climb will be substantially reduced, and in the case of many light twin engined aircraft this reduction may be as high as 90% or more of the original excess thrust horsepower, and in some cases, depending upon aircraft type, gross weight, temperature and aircraft configuration, a situation may occur where it will be impossible to maintain level flight should one engine fail.

Therefore, whilst it can be said that when in level flight the loss of one engine on a twin engined aircraft usually leaves the pilot a reasonably safe margin, this safety factor would be greatly reduced if the pilot needed to climb in this condition, as for example in a situation where an engine fails immediately after take-off.

It has already been stated that under conditions of asymmetric power, even with the propeller feathered and the aircraft in the clean configuration, an additional amount of drag will be present, as shown by the illustration in Fig 22, that is, the increased horsepower required is due to the increase in total drag that has occurred. Therefore in the take-off situation with landing gear and possibly flaps lowered, the drag could be such as to prevent even level flight from being achieved. In Fig 23 the drag with landing gear and flaps lowered is such that the available horsepower is insufficient for the aircraft to maintain height.

It might well be asked why the certification regulations (which are provided for reasons of safety) permit this state of affairs. The answer to this question is complex but it can be summed up as 'aeroplanes are built to sell', and cost effectiveness is a very real issue in any sales philosophy. Suffice to say that most light twin engined aircraft do have a climb capability on one engine, but it is relatively small. Therefore the training required in a pilot's conversion to multi engined aircraft involves explaining the problems and developing the pilot's competence to overcome them.

SINGLE ENGINE CEILING

This will be dependent upon the amount of excess thrust horsepower available when operating on one engine. The illustration in Fig 24 shows the approximate effect of altitude in relation to power curves. The solid lines show the horsepower required and the thrust available at sea level. The dashed lines show the effect of altitude upon these curves.

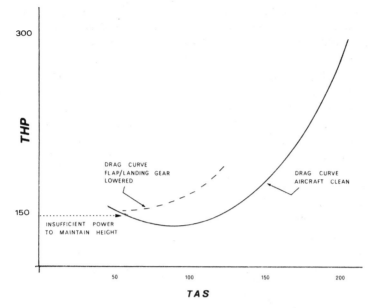

Fig 23

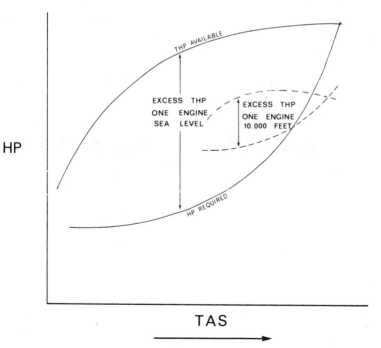

Fig 24

The reduction of horsepower available with normally aspirated engines is due to the lowering density with an increase in altitude, and at 10 000' the power available will be approximately one-third less than that achieved at sea level.

However, during asymmetric flight, the combined effect of altitude and the additional drag resulting from the loss in aerodynamic efficiency when operating on one engine, may in effect reduce the excess thrust horsepower at 10 000' by as much as two-thirds. Thus single engine ceilings of many twin engined aircraft are substantially lower than those obtained when both engines are operating (refer to Fig 24).

In relation to single engine ceilings and the information given in Flight/Owner's Manuals and Pilot's Operating Handbooks, there are two terms which may be used. These are single engine *Absolute Ceiling* and single engine *Service Ceiling*.

The term Absolute Ceiling is self-descriptive and needs no further clarification, but Service Ceiling is a term used to describe an altitude above which the aircraft's rate of climb on one engine drops below 50 feet per minute. It should be appreciated that for a pilot to maintain level flight for protracted periods, his aircraft will need the ability to climb at a rate of at least 50 feet per minute, otherwise even moderate turbulence producing downdraughts cannot be compensated for. Therefore when determining the practical single engine ceiling of an aircraft the Service Ceiling figures should be used.

Some aircraft manuals may not include specific tables or graphs showing the single engine service ceiling, but by noting the altitude at which the rate of climb drops to 50 feet per minute on one engine rate of climb tables or graphs, a practical single engine ceiling can be arrived at.

SINGLE ENGINE CLIMB DATA										
	SEA LEVEL 59°		2500 FT 50°F		5000 FT 41°F		7500 FT 32°F		10,000 FT 23°F	
Gross Weight Pounds	Best Climb KIAS	Rate of Climb Ft/Min	Best Climb KIAS	Rate of Climb Ft/Min	Best Climb KIAS	Rate of Climb Ft/Min	Best Climb KIAS	Rate of Climb Ft/Min	Best Climb KIAS	Rate of Climb Ft/Min
5500	106	370	103	265	100	156	97	48	94	-60
5100	102	448	99	340	96	230	93	122	90	13
4700	98	520	95	414	92	305	89	197	86	90

Fig 25

It should further be appreciated that if level flight in the clean configuration cannot be maintained at the best rate of climb speed for the aircraft's weight and altitude, then level flight at either a lower or higher speed will also be impossible. If an aircraft will not maintain altitude on one engine at V_{yse} this speed should be maintained whilst the aircraft descends slowly to its single engine ceiling where level flight can be re-established.

CRUISING, RANGE AND ENDURANCE

Cruising at altitude will present the least critical situation with regard to failure of one engine. However, once the engine has been shut down and the propeller feathered the question of fuel management must then be considered.

Apart from the fact that the normal range and endurance of the aircraft will be reduced due to the extra drag imposed by asymmetric flight, there will often be an additional constraint in that many twin engined aircraft have fuel systems in which certain fuel tanks, e.g. auxiliary and wing locker tanks, cannot be used for crossfeed purposes. This means that the total fuel aboard may not be available for the continuance of the planned flight. Aside from this, when the cause of failure cannot be ascertained, it may be that the engine failed due to contaminated fuel in the tank which was feeding it. If the fuel in this tank was to be used to feed the operating engine, then a serious risk of total power loss would occur. Therefore the procedures following an engine failure must include a review of the usable fuel quantity, the rate at which it is being used, e.g. a significantly higher power will be required from the operating engine, and the remaining distance to be flown. This review should determine the revised range and/or endurance available, and whether crossfeeding of fuel to an engine will be necessary.

ACCELERATION AND DECELERATION WITH ASYMMETRIC POWER

Most twin engined aircraft operating on one engine will lose between 80% and 90% of their performance capability with respect to rate of climb or acceleration. Although this must be appreciated when changing speed during the cruise condition, this performance aspect is most critical during the take-off, or missed approach situation.

The mathematics of climbing performance can be simply stated by the following: (*Note*: For SI equivalents see pages 68–9.)

$$\text{Rate of climb} = \frac{\text{Excess thrust horsepower} \times 33\,000}{\text{Aircraft weight (lb)}}$$

or,

$$\text{Excess thrust horsepower} = \frac{\text{Rate of climb} \times \text{weight (lb)}}{33\,000}$$

Taking a typical General Aviation twin engined aircraft as an example it can be seen from the performance figures given in the adjacent table that the excess thrust horsepower when operating on two engines is:

All Up Weight	Rate of Climb Two Engines f.p.m.	Rate of Climb One Engine f.p.m.	Vyse
5100 lbs	1670	318	100 Kts

$$\frac{1670 \times 5100}{33\ 000} = \frac{8517000}{33\ 000} = 258 \text{ excess thrust horsepower}$$

Resolving the equation for single engined operation will reduce the excess thrust horsepower as follows:

$$\frac{318 \times 5100}{33\ 000} = \frac{1621800}{33\ 000} = 49 \text{ excess thrust horsepower}$$

The percentage loss of performance can therefore be expressed as:

$$100 - \left(\frac{318}{1670} \times 100 \right) = 80 \cdot 9\%$$

Without going into detail regarding the mathematics involved in acceleration, it can be seen that an 80·9% loss in performance will have a very considerable effect upon the acceleration factor. Therefore even in the event of engine failure at safety speed when the pilot may reasonably decide to continue the climb out, he must appreciate that the aircraft's ability to accelerate will be drastically reduced, and the time taken to achieve V_{yse} will be substantially longer than the normal few seconds it takes when both engines are operating normally.

With respect to the climb out situation following failure of one engine, it must also be understood that due to the reduced acceleration and climb rate available the distance travelled whilst climbing to a safe height for manoeuvring will also be substantially increased, and if other adverse factors such as high temperature, high airfield elevation, light (or zero) wind condition, maximum all up weight, etc., are present the distance covered to reach a height of 500′ above the surface could be in order of 10 n.m.

The same situation will exist during a missed approach procedure if the approach speed has been allowed to drop below V_{yse}. It is for this reason that it is good practice to maintain an approach speed of at least V_{yse} until reaching Asymmetric Committal Height (Long Briefing, Sequence 2 of Part 2 on pages 132–3 refer).

Due to the far greater distance to be flown to reach a safe height, there may be a tendency on the part of the pilot to raise the nose of the aircraft in an attempt to climb more quickly. The reduction in airspeed resulting from this action could be dangerous, and the climbing speed must never be allowed to drop below the V_{xse}.

Because a number of different take-off and climb techniques could be employed during normal twin engined operation, the sensible pilot should plan for one which gives him the greatest advantage should engine failure occur during this phase of flight. For example, at one extreme a pilot could allow the airspeed to build up more quickly by initially maintaining level flight after lift off until the speed is in excess of the best rate of climb speed before commencing to climb. Alternatively he could lift the aircraft off the ground at the lowest speed possible and climb at the best (two engines operating) angle of climb speed.

If one considers the possibility of an engine failure during the take-off and initial climb phase, neither of these procedures would give the pilot the best opportunity of handling the situation.

The reason for this is that drag increases as the square of the speed, so that for any increase in speed over and above V_{yse} the greater will be the drag and the less will be the climb performance. Whilst the drag is increasing as the square of the velocity, the power required to maintain this increases as the cube of that velocity. Therefore a pilot who uses excessive speed during the initial climb out phase will be converting all the power energy into speed, and although excess speed can be converted into height, it is unlikely that this will be achieved efficiently as, by the time the pilot has controlled an engine failure situation, the excess speed may well have been dissipated.

From this it can be seen that power is best used to gain the maximum height at a safe airspeed as quickly as possible following take-off. This way the energy from the engines is being used most efficiently to gain height, and in the event of engine failure the pilot would have the option of trading height for speed if required. On the other hand, attempting to gain height more quickly at the expense of an efficient airspeed can be dangerous, because of control problems should an engine fail.

A good procedure is to lift off at Safety Speed (if this can be achieved on the ground in the particular aircraft), or at least V_{mca} + 5 knots, and climb (with both engines operating) at not less than V_{yse} and not more than V_y. When Safety Speed is not achievable on the ground, e.g. in order to avoid *wheelbarrowing*, or due to other factors, the aim should be to achieve Safety Speed by the time the aircraft is at 50' above the ground. This will result in the fastest acceleration consistent with gaining a reasonable height. The initial climb should be made at maximum permitted take-off power, following which maximum continuous climbing power should be selected, and the airspeed increased as required.

The consideration of deceleration with regard to asymmetric flight applies mainly to the landing approach stage of a flight. Due to the additional drag at any airspeed during asymmetric flight, more power will be needed to maintain a particular approach airspeed and descent rate. The additional drag will also lead to a more rapid deceleration and rate of sink than normal when power is reduced, and this could have a critical effect upon the final stages of an approach to landing. In these circumstances the pilot must be careful to anticipate any adverse conditions, e.g. wind shear effects, etc., in this phase of flight, and be prepared to counteract such effects by early application of power.

ZERO THRUST – DEFINITION AND PURPOSE

During training in asymmetric flight it will often be inconvenient or unsafe to have an engine feathered. Whilst it is obviously necessary to obtain practice in engine failure situations and procedures, it is also unwise to deliberately feather the propeller of one engine when the aircraft is at low altitudes. Past experience has shown that needless accidents have occurred due to critical situations developing, e.g. loss of power on the remaining engine during asymmetric training in the climb out or approach and landing phases.

To avoid this type of emergency when an aircraft is at low altitudes, and at the same time permit training to be conducted realistically, a particular power setting known as *Zero Thrust* can be established and set on the engine which is assumed to have failed. This will simulate the reduction in drag experienced when an engine is feathered.

DETERMINING ZERO THRUST FOR THE PARTICULAR AIRCRAFT TYPE

The power to use in the above circumstances is often shown in graph form in Aircraft Manuals. In the event that no information regarding this power setting is shown, a setting of 10 to 12 inches of manifold pressure will give an approximation of the zero thrust setting. Alternatively the procedure outlined in the Long Briefing, Sequence 1 of Part 2 of this Manual can be used to determine a suitable setting.

PERFORMANCE MATHEMATICS, SI EQUIVALENTS

$$\text{Rate of climb (metres/second)} = \frac{\text{Excess thrust power (kilowatts)} \times 1000}{\text{Aircraft mass (kg)} \times 9\cdot81 \ (\text{m/s}^2)}$$

or

$$\text{Excess thrust power (kW)} = \frac{\text{Rate of climb (m/s)} \times \text{Aircraft mass (kg)} \times 9\cdot81 \ (\text{m/s}^2)}{1000}$$

From the previous example, aircraft mass of 5100 lb   = 2313 kg
Rate of climb on two engines 1670 fpm = 8·483 m/s
Rate of climb on one engine   318 fpm = 1·615 m/s
Therefore when operating on two engines:

$$\text{Excess thrust power} = \frac{8 \cdot 483 \times 2313 \times 9 \cdot 81}{1000} = 192 \cdot 5 \text{ kW}$$

and for single engine operation:

$$\text{Excess thrust power} = \frac{1 \cdot 615 \times 2313 \times 9 \cdot 81}{1000} = 36 \cdot 7 \text{ kW}$$

Conversion factors:

1 lb = 0·4536 kg
1 m = 3·281 ft
1 hp = 0·746 kW

Propellers

The following information is of a revisionary nature only. For further details regarding propellers, see Manual No 3 of the Ground Training Series.

There are two principal types of propellers: fixed pitch and variable pitch. The fixed pitch propeller has no working parts and is used generally on low powered engines. The pitch of the blades is fixed and set at a pre-determined angle to achieve best results for a particular airspeed. Clearly such a propeller could not be feathered.

VARIABLE PITCH

Variable pitch propellers are designed so that the angle of the blades can be altered by the pilot while the aircraft is in flight. They are used in conjunction with a constant speed unit (CSU) and are therefore more commonly known as constant speed propellers. The use of a CSU enables the pitch of the propeller to be automatically adjusted for variations in engine power and aircraft speed, thereby enabling the propeller to operate more efficiently over a range of manifold pressures, rpm settings and airspeeds.

When variable pitch propellers are used the aircraft will also be equipped with a manifold pressure gauge unit for each engine. In the case of American manufactured engines, the manifold pressure gauges are calibrated in units of inches (Hg) similar to that used in a mercury barometer. Constant speed propellers may be electrically or hydraulically operated, and in multi engined aircraft are normally of the fully feathering type.

FEATHERING

A feathering propeller is one in which the blades can be turned until the blade chord lines are virtually parallel to the airflow and consequently no lift or thrust is produced. This stops the propeller windmilling in the airflow and although this action does not eliminate propeller drag it does reduce it to a minimum.

GENERAL PRINCIPLES AND PURPOSE OF FEATHERING

There are several different methods used in the construction and operation of CSUs and feathering mechanisms, and it is neither necessary nor practical to cover all the methods in this manual. A fairly common method is by utilizing counterweights attached to the blades. These counterweights are attached to the shank of each blade  such that when the propeller is spinning, the centre of mass of the counterweight tends towards the blade's plane of rotation, thus increasing the blade angle. The centrifugal twisting force produced by the counterweights is designed to be slightly greater than the blade's aerodynamic twisting force. A hydraulic linkage is then used to supplement the aerodynamic force in order to overcome the centrifugal force, thereby reducing the blade angle.

The rpm lever in the cockpit is then used as a datum to set the required rpm. If the propeller tends to increase its revolutions, e.g. as a result of increasing airspeed, the governor will open the oil passage and admit more oil pressure to the piston. This action will increase the blade angle slightly, coarsening the pitch, which will restore the rpm to its selected value.

If the propeller tends to decrease its revolutions, e.g. as a result of reducing airspeed, the governor will bleed oil pressure from the system permitting the centrifugal twisting moment of the blades to reduce the blade angle, fining or flattening the pitch until the selected rpm is restored.

On most twin engined propeller aircraft the feathering action is accomplished by moving the rpm lever out of the normal rpm range and through the feathering gate. This action will cause the governor to apply additional oil pressure to the system and rotate the propeller blades until their chord lines are parallel with the airflow. Another common method is one in which the effect of the counterweights attached to the base of the blades, together with the action of a powerful spring, is used to coarsen the blade angle and to feather the propeller. In this case oil pressure is only used to move the blades towards fine pitch and so if oil pressure is lost as a result of the engine failing, the propeller may still be feathered.

It should be noted that the preceding paragraphs outline general methods of CSU operation and although the basic principles discussed are common to many CSU systems used in twin engined aircraft, there are variations to these methods, and the particular procedures and operating limitations applicable to feathering action must be ascertained by reference to the aircraft manual. For example, some aircraft use feathering systems which will only operate provided the propeller is rotating at not less than 1000 rpm. This is because in this type of system a stop pin is activated at low rpm to avoid inadvertent feathering when the engines are shut down normally whilst on the ground.

Finally, whereas detailed information regarding feathering and unfeathering systems are not usually covered in Flight/Owner's Manuals or Pilot's Operating Handbooks, the actual drills and procedures are adequately covered and therefore no attempt is made to outline these in this manual.

Specific Aircraft Type

The contents of the Syllabus outlined under this heading are as follows:

Aeroplane and Engine Systems – Operation Normal, Abnormal and Emergency (details as applicable to type)
    Fuel System
    Oil System
    Oil Grade and Specification
    Ignition System
    Mixture Control System
    Propeller – Pitch Controls
    Cabin Heating and Ventilation Systems
    Pitot/Static System: Pressure Instruments
    Vacuum System: Gyroscopic Instruments and Limitations
    Electrical System, including gyroscopic Instruments as applicable
    Braking System
    Landing Gear
    Flying Controls, including Flaps
    Fire Extinguisher(s)
    Control Locks
    Hydraulic System
    De-icing System
    Pressurisation System
    Oxygen System
    Auto Pilot System
    Turbo Charging System
    Other Systems Particular to Type
    Limitations
    Airframe
        Load Factors
        Landing Gear and Flap – Limiting Speeds
        Manoeuvring Speed
        Rough Air Speed (V_{RA}/V_{NO})
        Maximum Speeds

Engines
  rpm and Manifold Pressure
  Temperatures and Pressures
Emergency Procedures
See Flight/Owner's Manual/Pilot's Operating Handbook for Type

The above items can only be covered by reference to the Flight/Owner's Manual or Pilot's Operating Handbook for the particular aircraft type, which must be studied in depth in order that a comprehensive understanding of the aircraft systems can be gained.

Additionally, the emergency procedures applicable to the operation of the aircraft and its systems must be thoroughly known by the pilot in order that failure or malfunction of aircraft systems, which could normally be handled competently and safely by the pilot, do not develop into critical situations as a result of ignorance of the correct procedures to adopt.

In relation to critical situations, it is not always appreciated by pilots that past records reveal engine failure as being the greatest single causal factor of serious General Aviation accidents. Additionally the records also show that the most common cause of engine failure is fuel starvation or exhaustion. Either of these are in the main attributable to lack of, or incorrect, pre-flight planning, or improper fuel management procedures.

Further to this, fuel contamination is also a significant factor in engine failures and must be guarded against by supervision of fuel uplifts and correctly applying fuel strainer valve operations.

Although the following operating practices are equally applicable to any aircraft they are considered of sufficient importance to warrant listing in this manual as a reminder to pilots converting onto multi engined aircraft.

- Know the limitations of the aircraft and its engines. Avoid operating in excess of those limitations. Be sure all engines are within acceptable operating parameters prior to take-off. Maintain proficiency in all engine and aircraft system operating procedures, including emergency procedures. Follow the manufacturer's operating instructions.

- Be completely familiar with the aircraft fuel system and fuel management procedures. Make adequate pre-flight preparations to ensure that sufficient clean fuel is on board the aircraft for the time to destination, plus an adequate reserve.

- Know and understand the positions of the fuel selector valves. Be familiar with the sequence for selecting the fuel tanks. Remember that many aircraft have fuel systems in which unused fuel from the carburettor is returned to the main tanks. If the auxiliary tanks are being used and the main tanks are full this returned fuel will be lost via the tank vents, thus reducing the anticipated range or endurance.

● Make a visual inspection to ensure that the fuel tanks are full. When flying with a partial fuel load, use a positive method to establish the quantity on board the aircraft before flight. Complete trust in fuel gauges has often resulted in critical in-flight situations.

● During pre-flight inspections, determine that all tank vent openings are clear of obstructions and undamaged. Check fuel flow from each tank prior to take-off. Be fully familiar with electric fuel pump operating procedures. When re-selecting tanks, monitor the fuel pressure until fuel flow is assured.

Another important point to note in relation to the systems fitted in twin engined aircraft concerns the fitment of de-icing boots or anti-icing systems. When this equipment is available it does not necessarily imply that the aircraft is cleared for flight into known icing conditions, and it should be appreciated that most models of light twin engined aircraft are not tested for such operations. Therefore, before operating into known icing conditions, the pilot will have to determine whether the aeroplane is properly equipped and approved for such a flight. The aircraft Flight Manual is the normal source for this information. The Owner's Manual or Pilot's Operating Handbook will usually provide information regarding flight into icing conditions, but this does not normally constitute approval of such flight operations.

The difference between the functions of de-icing and anti-icing systems should also be recognised by pilots. A de-icing system used at the wrong time may negate its usefulness. For example, a thin coat of ice may be flexible and inflation of de-icing boots will in this case merely stretch the ice and form a shell within which the boots would then operate without any effect. It is therefore important to allow the ice to build up to a point where expansion of the boots will break it up. On the other hand, anti-icing equipment is designed to be actuated in anticipation of icing, and may be ineffective if activated after ice has accumulated.

WEIGHT AND BALANCE

The basic principles concerning weight and balance, together with the methods of calculation, are covered in the basic Private Pilot Syllabus, The AOPA Student Manual, and Technical Manual No 3 of the Ground Subject Training series.

It will nevertheless also be important to study the Flight/Owner's Manual/Pilot's Operating Handbook for the particular aircraft type, and practise the solution of weight and balance problems for varying fuel, passenger and baggage weights.

Weight and Performance

This aspect of twin engined aircraft operation should be studied in conjunction with the Weight and Performance – General Provisions of the Air Navigation (General) Regulations, BCARs and the Flight/ Owner's Manual or Pilot's Operating Handbook for the aircraft type.

The Air Navigation (General) Regulations include the following terms and definitions:

TAKE-OFF RUN AVAILABLE (TORA)

The take-off run available means the distance from the point on the surface of the aerodrome at which the aeroplane can commence its take-off run to the nearest point in the direction of take-off at which the surface of the aerodrome is incapable of bearing the weight of the aeroplane under normal operating conditions.

EMERGENCY DISTANCE AVAILABLE (EDA)

The emergency distance available means the distance from the point on the surface of the aerodrome at which the aeroplane can commence its take-off run to the nearest point in the direction of take-off at which the aeroplane cannot roll over the surface of the aerodrome and be brought to rest in an emergency. (ICAO uses the term *Accelerate– Stop Distance.*)

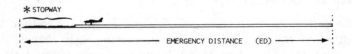

TAKE-OFF DISTANCE AVAILABLE (TODA)

The take-off distance available means either the distance from the point on the surface of the aerodrome at which the aeroplane can commence its take-off run to the nearest obstacle in the direction of take-off projecting above the surface of the aerodrome and capable of affecting the safety of the aeroplane, or one and one-half times the take-off run available, whichever is the less.

LANDING DISTANCE AVAILABLE (LDA)
The landing distance available means the distance from the point on the surface of the aerodrome above which the aeroplane can be deemed to commence its landing, having regard to the obstructions in its approach path, i.e. the threshold, to the nearest point in the direction of landing at which the surface of the aerodrome is incapable of bearing the weight of the aeroplane under normal operating conditions. Note that the landing threshold may be displaced from the start of the TORA.

*The terms *Stopway* and *Clearway* are explained below, under 'Aerodrome Distances'.

AERODROME DISTANCES – CAP 168 REQUIREMENTS (UK)
In the UK, the aerodrome licensing requirements of the Civil Air Publication 168 give detailed guidance to aerodrome owners on the criteria to be used for the determination of *Declared Distances* which are shown in the UK Air Pilot. The basic terms TORA, EDA, TODA, and LDA as illustrated in CAP 168 are shown in Fig 26. These correspond with the definitions in the Regulations, but CAP 168 goes on to specify in greater detail the criteria which govern the *Clearway* and *Stopway* distances which have been added to the runway length in this instance in order to obtain TODA and EDA respectively. The two terms are broadly defined in CAP 168 as follows:

Stopway   A Stopway may be regarded as an extension of the runway and as being provided for infrequent use. It affords an additional length, in excess of the runway itself, to bring an aeroplane to a stop without injury to the occupants or damage to the aircraft. Since it is for occasional use only it is not necessary for it to have the same weight bearing or wearing qualities of the runway.

Clearway   Clearway provides an area over which an aircraft can fly from lift-off to the prescribed height over the first

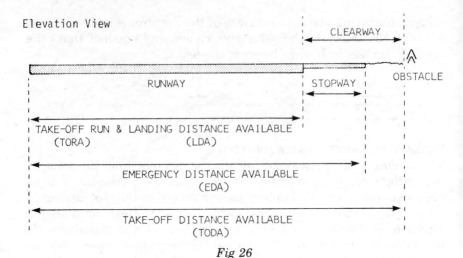

Fig 26

obstruction. (The published TODA may include Clearway, but aircraft in Groups C, D and E are not permitted to take account of take-off distance in excess of the ED.)

The method of showing the TORA, ED, TODA and LDA in the UK Air Pilot is illustrated in Fig 27 (item 1).

Also to be taken into account in the performance requirements for all aeroplanes is the slope of TORA, EDA, TODA and the LDA.

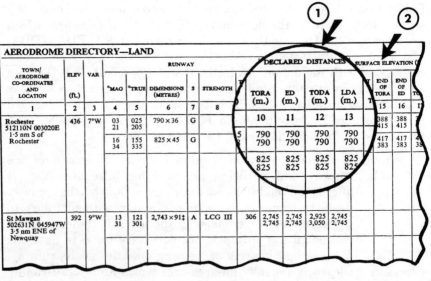

Fig. 27

Factored performance data in Flight Manuals includes slope scheduled as a percentage gradient. This is calculated from the information in the UK Air Pilot (see Fig 27, item 2), remembering that elevations are usually expressed in *feet above mean sea level* and horizontal distances are given in *metres*.

In the case of an unmarked take-off and landing strip, the approximate direction of which is shown in the AGA Section of the UK Air Pilot, the distance quoted will be the equivalent to that of a marked runway within the strip.

FLIGHT PLANNING CONSIDERATIONS

For those aeroplanes with approved Flight Manuals, i.e. Manuals containing data for aeroplanes used for Public Transport, safety factors have normally been included in the data presented, but in any case the pilot should ensure the following for safe flight during the take-off and landing stages:

1. The take-off run required should not exceed the take-off run available.

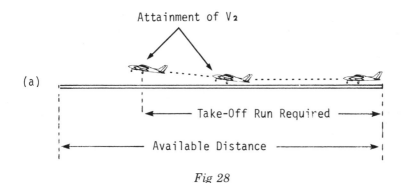

Fig 28

Take-Off Run Required is defined in BCARs, for Groups C and D aircraft as:

'The Take-Off Run Required shall be 1·15 times the gross horizontal distance to accelerate on a dry hard surface from the starting point and to attain a speed equal to V_2, when the aeroplane is held on or near the ground'

The Take-Off Distance required should not exceed the take-off distance available.

The Take-Off Distance required should also not exceed the emergency distance available.

The take-off flight path should at all times clear any obstacle by a vertical interval of at least 35' in straight flight, and by 50' in turning flight.

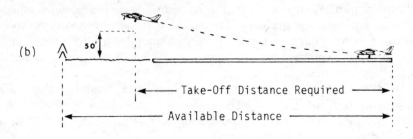

(b)

Take-Off Distance Required

Available Distance

Fig. 29

The Landing Distance required should not exceed the landing distance available.

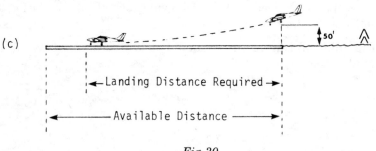

(c)

Landing Distance Required

Available Distance

Fig 30

2. For aeroplane types where *gross or measured distances* are given in the performance data, i.e. *unfactored distances*, it should be ensured that the *gross or measured landing distances* from 50' do not exceed 70% of the landing distance available.

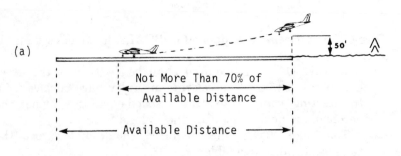

(a)

Not More Than 70% of
Available Distance

Available Distance

Fig. 31

The *gross or measured* Take-Off Distance to 50' should neither exceed 75% of the take-off distance available, nor 75% of the emergency distance available.

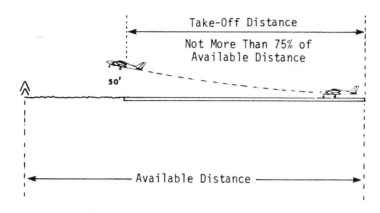

Fig 32

The take-off and landing weights should not exceed the maximum weights (WAT limits) specified for the altitude and air temperature of the relevant aerodrome.

FACTORS AFFECTING FIELD AND CLIMB PERFORMANCE

The main factors affecting performance comprise weather, terrain, and aircraft state, and before any flight the pilot must take the following into account:

- Aircraft all up weight (a 10% increase in weight results in a 20% increase in the take-off run)
- Airfield altitude and temperature at departure and destination (1000' amsl adds 10% to the take-off run and 10° C above ISA can add at least 12% to the take-off run)
- Take-off distance available and whether the runway is unpaved, uphill, wet, covered with long grass, soft or snow covered (long grass, soft ground or snow can add 25% to the take-off run and in some cases can even prevent lift off speed being attained). A runway slope of 2% uphill can add 10% to the take-off run
- Reported wind at departure and forecast wind at destination (a tailwind component that is 10% of the lift off speed will increase the take-off run by 20%, whilst a headwind component 10% of the lift off speed will decrease it by 20%)
- Obstacles in the flight path after take-off
- Obstacles en route
- Landing distance available and whether the landing runway is downhill, wet, icy or snow covered

The consequences of one engine failing at any stage during the flight must also be considered.

The foregoing information on flight planning is largely based upon the advice contained in *Aeronautical Information Circular* No 52(76) 1985. This circular will be updated from time to time and pilots should follow the advice it contains.

An important aspect which has to be considered and which relates to Emergency Distance is the possibility of an engine failing at a critical stage of the take-off. To cater for this contingency, most Owner's Manuals and Pilot's Operating Handbooks give information expressed in terms of *Accelerate–Stop, Accelerate–Go* distance, or in terms of *Refusal Speed* or *Decision Speed*, above which the aircraft cannot be stopped within the remaining distance available, if the pilot elects to discontinue the take-off for any reason.

Data contained in CAA approved Flight Manuals for aircraft in performance Groups C, D and E used on Public Transport operations does not include this information as an acceptable safety level is achieved by other airworthiness and operational restrictions.

ACCELERATE–STOP DISTANCE CONSIDERATIONS

The purpose of Accelerate–Stop Distance charts is to enable the pilot to predict the distance required to accelerate the aircraft to lift-off speed, experience an engine failure, then close the throttles and bring the aircraft to a complete stop using heavy braking.

If the available Emergency Distance exceeds this figure and an engine failure occurs before lift-off speed, it would theoretically be possible for the aircraft to be stopped within the remaining distance.

When the Accelerate–Stop distance required is greater than the Emergency Distance available, then the aircraft cannot be safely stopped after reaching lift-off speed. In this event a pilot should, before flight, reduce the aircraft weight. Alternatively, consideration should be given to using a different runway where the Emergency Distance is greater, or waiting for more favourable take-off conditions, e.g. a stronger headwind component, lower temperature, etc.

Using the Accelerate–Stop Distance chart illustrated in Fig 33 it can be seen that the aircraft would need to have 600 metres available to accelerate to 80 knots and then with the throttles closed and using heavy braking, stop within the remaining distance available. If an engine failure occurred at V_{me}, then an Emergency Distance of 700 metres would be needed to allow the aircraft to be stopped with safety.

An important point to bear in mind when making calculations of this nature is that the Accelerate–Stop Distance shown in Owner's Manuals or Pilot's Operating Handbooks do not usually allow for the element of surprise and the time taken for the pilot to complete the correct procedure.

Another fact to remember when deciding whether an aircraft can be safely stopped in the remaining distance available is that some aircraft manuals quote the Accelerate–Stop Distances assuming that

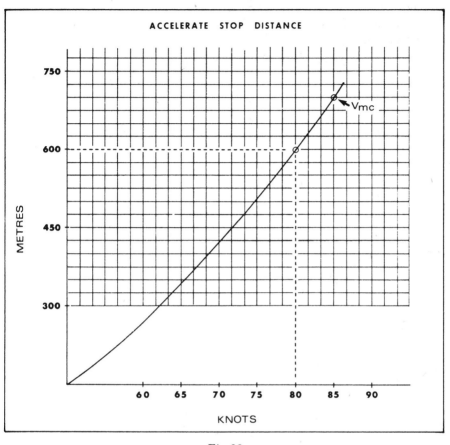

Fig 33

the take-off commences from the very end of the runway and that full power is applied before the brakes are released and the take-off run commenced. As this procedure is not normally employed during take-off, the Accelerate–Stop distances quoted will usually be shorter than those applicable to the normal take-off procedure. In view of this it would therefore be prudent to increase the figures calculated from Owner's Manuals and Pilot's Operating Handbooks which contain unfactored data. One method is to use the V_{xse} as a datum speed and then add 2% to the calculated Accelerate–Stop Distance for each knot of difference between the decision speed and the V_{xse}.

The further items which appear in the AOPA Multi Engine Syllabus under the heading of WAT Limitations are included there so that a pilot will more fully appreciate the effects of the various factors upon take-off and landing performance. Therefore it would be of value to obtain practice in the use of the Specimen Performance Charts,

Groups C or E, as published by the Civil Aviation Authority, Airworthiness Division, and available from the CAA, Greville House, Cheltenham, England.

FLIGHT SYLLABUS

Conversion to Twin Engined Aircraft

Long Briefings

Part 1 Normal Flight: Sequence 1

Long Briefing

OBJECTIVES

To acquaint the student with the specific aircraft being used for training in relation to the handling procedures for multi engined aircraft. Essentially this period is confined to the operation of the various controls and systems, and in practice at handling the aircraft in straight and level flight.

The following items will be covered during this briefing:

Aircraft Familiarisation
Pre-Flight Preparation and Aircraft Inspection
Starting Up Procedures
Parking Area Procedures
Taxying
Pre Take-Off Procedures
The Take-Off and Initial Climb
Introduction to the Effects of the Various Controls and Systems
Emergency Drills (not including engine failure)
Straight and Level Flight
Circuit Joining, Approach and Landing. A Review of Drills and Procedures

Due to the many variations which occur between multi engined aircraft, their systems, and the operation of such systems, these briefing notes cannot cater for individual types of aircraft. They are therefore confined to a systematic coverage of the general points which arise during conversion onto multi engined aircraft.

AIRCRAFT FAMILIARISATION

Prior to the initial flight the student will be introduced to the aircraft Flight/Owner's Manual/Pilot's Operating Handbook. This document must be studied sufficiently to ensure that an adequate knowledge is obtained of the aircraft, its controls and instrument layout, and the operation of its various systems.

During the initial stage of training, the student must be introduced

87

to, and carry out, practical weight and balance calculations using the information contained in the Weight and Balance Schedule and the aircraft manual.

Due to the wider number of loading options for passengers, baggage and fuel, it is extremely important to carry out calculations relating to high payloads and short range as well as low payloads and longer range.

This practice is vital to ensure the student appreciates that it is not always possible to operate safely if all passenger seats and baggage areas are filled, when carrying the maximum load of fuel in the tanks.

PRE-FLIGHT PROCEDURES

This section of the aircraft manual should be reviewed, and it will be seen that the number of internal and external items which must be checked during the pre-flight inspection and start up procedures are considerably greater than those in a single engined aircraft. This makes the use of a checklist essential, in order to avoid items being missed or forgotten.

TAXYING

Provided both engines are operating normally, the twin engined aeroplane handles in much the same way as a single engined aeroplane. However, because it is larger and heavier than its single engined counterpart, the rudder controls will require greater pressures, and the inertia effects will be more marked. Extra time, and a greater distance, will therefore be needed to carry out manoeuvres. These considerations will apply both on the ground and in the air.

STARTING, CONTROL OF SPEED AND STOPPING

Due to the greater wing span and fuselage length, additional care will be necessary when manoeuvring, particularly in the parking area. A higher power will be required to initiate movement, and therefore greater care must be used to prevent slipstream effects from damaging smaller aircraft and from blowing debris, leaves, etc., into open hangar doors.

Caution must also be used to avoid taxying too fast as the increased wing span makes it more difficult to judge clearance from nearby obstacles, and the greater aircraft weight and increased inertia will require an earlier reduction of power, and firmer braking action to bring the aircraft to a stop.

CONTROL OF DIRECTION AND TURNING

Most twin engined aircraft are equipped with a nosewheel linked to the rudder pedals, and therefore a combination of rudder and differential braking is used for directional control.

Turning in Confined Spaces

Differential power can also be utilised to assist directional control when brisk crosswinds prevail, or when manoeuvring is being carried out in confined areas. When using differential power in confined spaces particular care must be exercised to avoid locking a mainwheel and so placing unacceptable stresses on the tyre sidewalls.

When using narrow taxyways it must also be remembered that the main wheels of a twin engined aircraft are set further apart, and extra care should be taken to avoid a wheel coming off the taxyway onto soft ground. This will particularly apply when turning around sharp bends.

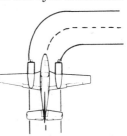

During taxying the normal instrument serviceability checks should be carried out, and the student should also check that he can apply full rudder and that it is free over its entire travel.

When stopping the aircraft preparatory to carrying out the power and system checks, it is important to bring the aircraft to a stop with the nosewheel aligned fore and aft, otherwise considerable lateral stress can be placed upon the nosewheel gear assembly when high power is applied.

PRE TAKE-OFF PROCEDURES

POWER AND SYSTEM CHECKS

The need for these checks to be carried out is exactly the same as for single engined aircraft, but due to the greater slipstream effects, additional care must be used to ensure that the aircraft is positioned with the tailplane pointing well away from other aircraft, and in an area which is clear of loose stones, etc.

In multi engined aircraft certain systems are duplicated for each engine, and so the number of checks to be done will be greater. Therefore a checklist will be required to ensure that all the power  and system checks are implemented. Self discipline must be used to avoid hurrying or taking short cuts through these checks.

PRE TAKE-OFF CHECKS
These should be completed with reference to the checklist for the particular aircraft type. Prior to requesting take-off clearance, a review of the important speeds such as V_{mca}, Safety Speed, and V_{yse}, should be made.

Other pertinent speeds will also have to be memorised. These are: the speed to lift the nosewheel, the lift-off speed, the best rate of climb speed with both engines operating (V_y), and the best angle of climb speed with both engines operating (V_x). Another significant speed to have in mind at this stage would be the maximum speed permitted for flight with the landing gear extended (V_{le}).

THE TAKE-OFF AND INITIAL CLIMB

Once ATC clearance has been received the aircraft should be lined up in the centre of the runway and held stationary against the brakes until approximately 50% power has been applied. This will allow the pilot to confirm that the engines are developing their power smoothly and symmetrically, and that the fuel flows or pressures are registering correctly.

INTO WIND TAKE-OFF
When the brakes are released, control of direction is achieved normally through the use of the rudder pedals, and at the same time a slight back pressure is applied to the control column.

When full power has been applied, brief reference should be made to the engine instruments and air speed indicator to ensure that the engines are developing full power, and that the oil temperatures, pressures, cylinder head temperatures, fuel flow or fuel pressure gauges, and air speed indicator are all giving normal indications.

At the recommended speed for the aircraft type

the nosewheel should be raised off the runway by application of additional back pressure.

Upon achieving the recommended lift-off speed, rotation should be made firmly and positively. The initial attitude should be one which permits a safe but rapid increase of speed through V_2, that is, an attitude to achieve a flight path very nearly parallel with the ground. As Safety Speed, V_2, is passed and at a height of about 50', the brakes should be momentarily applied and the landing gear selected up. When taking off on long runways it is good practice to delay retracting the landing gear until a point is reached where a wheels down forced landing on the runway (in the event of one engine failing) would be impractical.

On some light twins it is possible to achieve V_2 before the moment of rotation without holding the aeroplane down unduly, in a way likely to stress the nosewheel leg or lead to 'wheelbarrowing'. This procedure gives the best possible protection against engine failure problems, as discussed later in Part 2 of these Long Briefings. However, in the case of those light twin engined aircraft which cannot be operated in this way, a pilot must accept that there is a risk from engine failure during the acceleration from lift off to safety speed and his aim should be to keep the risk to a minimum, by achieving V_2 as quickly as possible.

When flaps have been used for the take-off these should be retracted as soon as a safe height has been reached and certainly before V_{fe}. After sufficient height has been gained the airspeed may be increased for a cruise climb, and above 1000' agl the electric fuel pumps may be switched 'off' (when applicable for the aircraft type).

When switching off fuel pumps in a twin engined aircraft, it is good procedure to select them off individually, pausing for a few seconds between each selection to note that the fuel flow or fuel pressure is being maintained for the relevant engine.

CROSSWIND TAKE-OFF

When a significant crosswind is present during the take-off run, it will often be an advantage to lead slightly with the appropriate throttle, i.e. the throttle on the windward side, whilst increasing power after the brakes have been released. This will assist directional control in the early stages of the take-off run.

EFFECTS OF CONTROLS

A convenient and orderly way to introduce the single engined pilot to the various controls of a twin engined aircraft during flight is to follow in a general fashion the sequence of the basic 'Effects of Controls' exercise, with the aim of introducing the increased control pressures required to operate the primary controls and illustrating the rate and amount of change to the attitude in pitch, and airspeed, when operating such items as flaps, landing gear, power and trimming controls, etc.

PRIMARY AND TRIMMING CONTROLS

When the operating altitude is reached, the aircraft should be set up for straight and level flight and the student asked to fly the aircraft for a short while in order to determine the control pressures required to move the elevators, ailerons and rudder, and to appreciate the aircraft's rate of response to these pressures. Following this the trimming controls should be operated to determine the sense of their movement and the degree of effectiveness for the amount of movement.

ENGINE CONTROLS

For pilots who have not flown aircraft with constant speed propellers it will be necessary to note that the pitch levers control the rpm, and the throttles control the manifold pressures which are normally indicated on the gauges in inches (Hg). A little difficulty is usually experienced at first in cross referring to the correct gauges, manifold pressure (MP) or rpm when moving the throttles and pitch levers, but with a little practice this problem is soon overcome.

In connection with the selection of the appropriate MP or rpm settings, care must be used to avoid overboosting, i.e. setting too high a manifold pressure for too low an rpm. On those aircraft which have green arc segments on the MP and rpm gauges the normal practice is to ensure that the MP is not increased beyond the top of the green arc on the MP gauge unless the rpm is above the green arc on the rpm gauge. Therefore, when making significant power increases the pitch controls should be moved first, followed by the throttles, and when reducing power the throttles are brought back first, followed by the rpm.

SYNCHRONISING THE ENGINES

Although the use of the MP and rpm gauges will allow a pilot to select the same power on each engine reasonably accurately, it will not be possible to use these instruments to synchronise the engines completely. The result of this is that a differential noise is heard from the engines, and it will be necessary to make a final adjustment of the rpm to synchronise the engines and so avoid this pulsating effect.

To do this, gently move any one pitch lever forward or backward. If the engine beat speeds up (shortens), it indicates the wrong direction of movement, if the engine beat slows down (lengthens), it indicates that the movement is in the right direction, and it will then only be necessary to continue to move the pitch lever in the same direction until a constant engine noise is obtained. The ability to synchronise the engines quickly and efficiently will only be developed by constant practice.

FLAP OPERATION

The method of operating the flaps, together with the flap position presentation, and the approximate cycling times, will have been covered on the ground and during the pre-flight procedures.

First ensure that the airspeed is within the flap operating range and then, with the aircraft in a trimmed condition, operate the flap through the various positions noting the direction in which the aircraft changes attitude in pitch, and the amount and rate of change.

Return the aircraft to the level flight attitude, and retrim after each flap selection and note the difference in airspeed. Re-select flaps up in stages, and note the pitch change force which occurs during each selection.

LANDING GEAR OPERATION

Reduce the airspeed to below the V_{le} and re-trim the aircraft. Select landing gear down and note any change of attitude in pitch. Return the aircraft to the original flight attitude, re-trim and note the decrease in airspeed resulting from the increased drag. During this period the indications of landing gear position, i.e. locked up, cycling, and locked down, should be noted.

USE OF THE FUEL SYSTEM DURING FLIGHT

The fuel systems of multi engined aircraft are usually more complex than those of single engined aircraft, and due to the many variations of installation and methods of operation, it is not possible to include more than a few brief comments on fuel procedures in this manual.

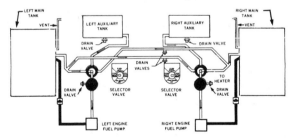

The methods of tank selection including the use of fuel gauge indications and electric fuel pumps when re-selecting tanks must be covered in relation to the training aircraft. It is important to adhere to the fuel tank selection procedures specified in the aircraft manual.

Most twin engined aircraft have fuel systems which incorporate a crossfeed facility, i.e. the ability to run the left engine from the right tank and vice versa. However, it may not be possible to crossfeed from auxiliary or other additional tanks if these are installed.

MIXTURE CONTROL

The greater the power output of a particular engine, the greater its rate of fuel consumption. Therefore with more powerful engines the use of mixture control assumes greater importance.

In order to assist the pilot with fuel management, larger engines are normally equipped with instruments indicating rate of fuel flow, which can then be adjusted with the mixture control to meet the figures shown in the aircraft manual for various power settings.

An exhaust gas analyser may also be fitted which permits the pilot to adjust the mixture, and so produce the higher combustion temperatures which result from a more efficient and economical use of fuel. The aircraft manual will have to be consulted in order to determine the correct method of achieving economical fuel consumption through the use of the exhaust gas temperature gauges.

USE OF ALTERNATE AIR OR CARBURETTOR HEAT CONTROLS

There are two methods of preventing or clearing icing in the carburettor system. Low power engines are usually equipped with a carburettor heating system in which hot air is directed into the induction intake from a heat exchanger or exhaust muff. On higher power engines, the usual method is to direct air from a source other than the main induction intake. This supply of air is normally taken from an inlet port within the engine cowling, from which drier and warmer air is obtained.

When using either of these systems the maximum power normally available from the engines will be slightly reduced and the fuel/air mixture will be enriched. The method of operating these systems will be detailed in the aircraft manual.

Twin engined aircraft are often equipped with carburettor heat gauges to indicate the temperature of the air in the vicinity of the throttle valves: such gauges are usually colour coded to give a clear indication of the possibility of ice formation.

OPERATION OF COWL FLAPS AND COOLING GILLS

To give the pilot some control over the cylinder head temperatures, all high power engines are equipped with shutters (flaps or gills) which can be set to vary the supply of cooling air passing into and out of the engine bay. Many different types of installation are in use and the pilot will need to acquaint himself with the methods of operation of these systems and also the recommended temperatures for the particular make of engine. The cylinder head temperature gauges are normally colour coded and can be interpreted simply and quickly.

OPERATION OF CABIN HEATING AND VENTILATION SYSTEMS
Due to the larger cabin area in twin engined aircraft, combustion type heaters are now widely used. Essentially they consist of a petrol burning heater unit, combustion air blower, ventilation air blower and a control unit. The control unit provides for selection of hot or cold air to the cabin and the windshield.

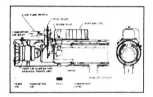

OTHER SYSTEMS AS APPLICABLE TO TYPE
Due to the differences which exist between twin engined aircraft in relation to the number and type of systems with which they are equipped, reference must be made to the particular aircraft manual to determine the systems available and methods of operation.

EMERGENCY DRILLS AND PROCEDURES

These will have to be conducted in accordance with the information given in the particular aircraft manual. Due to the many differences between aircraft, it is not possible to learn a standard method of drills and procedures which are applicable to all aircraft types. It will therefore be necessary to study the procedures detailed in the 'Emergency Procedures' section of the relevant Flight/Owner's Manual/Pilot's Operating Handbook for type.

STRAIGHT AND LEVEL FLIGHT

The combinations of manifold pressure and rpm used to achieve cruising conditions in level flight vary for different aircraft types and the power settings applicable to the aircraft used for training will apply for this demonstration and practice.

It will nevertheless be important to bear in mind that in some aircraft manuals it is recommended that the sustained use of a certain rpm range be avoided. This is usually due to unacceptable engine vibration within this range, and for the convenience of the pilot it is often shown by a yellow (or sometimes red) band on the tachometer.

Note: A yellow band just below the red (never exceed) line on the tachometer is being increasingly adopted to remind the pilot about noise avoidance when the aircraft is near the ground. This band should not be mistaken for the vibration range.

In order for a pilot to be fully competent at handling the specific aircraft in level flight at different configurations and power settings, it will be necessary for him to practise operating the flaps and landing gear whilst maintaining altitude and airspeed. Therefore once the pilot has become proficient at maintaining straight and level flight at various power settings and airspeeds he should practise maintaining altitude and/or airspeed whilst altering the flight configuration.

A simple routine for this exercise is to reduce the airspeed to within the flap operating range and select different flap positions whilst maintaining straight and level flight, and increasing power to maintain a constant airspeed. The resulting attitude change in pitch should be noted for each flap position. The same routine should be used for level flight with the landing gear lowered.

When converting onto a new type of multi engined aircraft it will be useful to know the difference in drag values between the landing gear and flaps in the lowered position. Such information could be important during an approach to landing, should the need to go around arise when flying on one engine. Knowledge of whether the flaps or landing gear produce the most drag under these circumstances may enable the pilot to determine the best order in which to clean up the aircraft in order to quickly improve its single engine performance in critical circumstances. Nevertheless, when the aircraft manual states the order in which drag should be removed during a 'go around', these recommendations should be followed.

PERFORMANCE CONSIDERATIONS – RANGE AND ENDURANCE
The range of any aircraft will be dependent upon the amount of fuel available, the aircraft weight, the use of mixture control, the power being used, the altitude flown, and the prevailing wind.

These considerations clearly have no fixed value, and so will vary on different flights. The aircraft manual will have to be consulted, and the best power settings and altitudes used to fit the situation.

In relation to the amount of MP and rpm to be used for efficiency, it can be generally stated that high MP and low rpm will normally lead to the most efficient fuel consumption. This is because at higher rpm there will inevitably be higher friction power losses in the engine and the engine driven ancillary systems, e.g. alternators, pumps, etc. Thus whenever the selected rpm is greater than that required for operational efficiency, a greater fuel consumption will occur. Further to this, the use of higher manifold pressure will lead to smaller throttle valve restrictions and greater induction efficiency.

In order to achieve the best range or endurance, it will be necessary to use the mixture control system throughout the flight, as savings in fuel consumption of up to 20% can be attained when the mixture control is used correctly,

CIRCUIT RE-JOINING, APPROACH AND LANDING

At this stage, an introduction to the method of positioning the aircraft into the circuit, and a review of the appropriate cockpit drills and circuit procedures will be made. This will also include a demonstration of a normal circuit, approach and landing. The detailed briefing covering normal circuits, approaches and landings is given in Part 1, Sequence 3.

RUNNING DOWN AND SWITCHING OFF

This procedure should be conducted in accordance with the information given in the aircraft manual and checklist.

AIRMANSHIP (ALL SEQUENCES)

It will be important to consider the need for carrying out Weight and Balance and Weight and Performance calculations prior to flight.

Due to the complexity and number of systems, the greater instrumentation and increased workloads on the pilot, including the requirement to use checklists, more time will be spent looking inside the cockpit. Therefore greater care will be required in ensuring that an adequate 'Lookout' is maintained.

The higher operating airspeeds associated with multi engined aircraft will also mean that greater anticipation will be needed when estimating the relative position of cloud, controlled airspace and similar areas, and other aircraft. The latter will be particularly important in relation to positioning the aircraft safely when in the traffic pattern.

Part 1   Normal Flight: Sequence 2

Long Briefing

OBJECTIVES

To give the pilot practice and where necessary to demonstrate to him the control and handling of a twin engined aircraft during climbing, turning and descending manoeuvres (including the emergency descent procedures), and to introduce the additional considerations related to stalling and advanced turning.

The following items will be covered during this briefing:

Revision of Pre-Flight Procedures
Taxying – Emergency Drills
Take-Off and Initial Climb
Climbing
Altimeter Setting Procedures (revision)
Descending (including Emergency Descent Procedures)
Turning, Medium Level, Climbing and Descending Turns
Slow Flight and Stalling
Advanced Turning
Instrument Appreciation (all normal manoeuvres)

TAXYING – EMERGENCY DRILLS

Should loss of braking or nosewheel steering failure occur, the procedure is the same as for single engined aircraft. It is, however, even more important not to continue taxying in these circumstances, as the greater weight and therefore greater inertia of the aircraft requires a longer stopping distance. Additionally, any malfunction of the nosewheel steering will lead to greater stresses being placed on the nosewheel assembly.

CLIMBING

All the basic requirements for entering, maintaining, and levelling off from a climb will apply. There are, however, some additional points to be borne in mind and these are:

- The need to increase the rpm before opening the throttles to climbing power.
- Care should be taken not to exceed the recommended climbing rpm and manifold pressure.
- Due to the greater climb rates of twin engined aircraft extra care must be taken to plan the climb direction to avoid entering the base of controlled airspace, or unintentionally entering cloud at this stage of conversion training.
- In the case of normally aspirated engines, the manifold pressure will reduce with increase of altitude and the throttles will therefore have to be readjusted at intervals during the climb, until they are fully forward. At this stage the aircraft will have reached an altitude known as 'full throttle height', and thereafter it will not be possible to maintain the former climbing power. This will lead to a gradual but positive drop in the aircraft's rate of climb.

In the case of supercharged or turbocharged engines, the manifold pressure will be maintained to considerably higher altitudes.

LEVELLING OFF FROM THE CLIMB

This is done in the normal manner but the manifold pressure should be set before reducing the rpm. In the case of normally aspirated engines the MP will change when the rpm is reduced, therefore a further MP adjustment will be necessary to obtain the required power.

EFFECT OF FLAPS ON THE CLIMB

This particular practice should be carried out at a reasonably low altitude (not above 1500′) so that the effect of flaps on climb performance during a climb immediately after take-off can be noted.

Practice will be given in the handling of the aircraft whilst raising the flaps in stages. This practice is to simulate the implementation of a 'go round again' procedure.

EN-ROUTE CLIMB (CRUISE CLIMB)

A twin engined aircraft allows greater flexibility of power and airspeed selection during a cruise climb. Normally the climbing speed can be increased by up to 25% without a significant reduction in the rate of climb.

MAXIMUM ANGLE OF CLIMB

At least one climb should be conducted at V_x so that the pilot can acquaint himself with the required attitude for a climb at this airspeed.

ALTIMETER SETTING PROCEDURES

Most twin engined aircraft are equipped with two altimeters, thereby giving the pilot the facility of setting the airfield QFE as well as the QNH. Once airborne and depending upon the altitude to be flown, the altimeters can be changed to the datums of the Area QNH and the Standard Setting 1013 mb respectively, thus giving immediate reference for obstruction clearance as well as flight levels.

A further point is that during this conversion training a student may for the first time find himself operating at altitudes in excess of 10 000′ amsl. It will therefore be necessary to appreciate this when interpreting altimeter readings, e.g. the need to check the 10 000′ needle and the visual indications of the striped 'altimeter warning segment' when climbing above or descending below 10 000′.

Surface Level	4000′	10.050′
Full Stripe Segment	Part Stripe Segment	No Stripes
Showing	Showing	Showing

PROLONGED CLIMB AND USE OF THE COWL FLAPS OR GILLS

The operation of high performance engines will require more frequent monitoring of the engine oil temperature and pressure gauges, and there will be an increased need to check the cylinder head temperatures, particularly during prolonged climbs, or at any time when mixture control procedures are being used.

The usual method of increasing the cooling air to the cylinders is to open the cooling flaps or gills in order to keep the cylinder head temperatures within the limits shown by the colour coding on the cylinder head temperature gauges, and as recommended in the aircraft manual.

Should these temperatures continue to rise after the cooling flaps or gills have been fully opened, it will be necessary to reduce power, or increase airspeed, or enrich the mixture, or employ a combination of all three.

DESCENDING

Gliding descents are not normally made in twin engined aircraft because of the need to prevent rapid cooling of the higher performance engines. A powered descent is therefore normal, and it can be conducted at various combinations of manifold pressure and rpm to give the required rate of descent. It will, however, be advisable to avoid rpm settings which are below the green arcs shown on the tachometer gauges.

PRE DESCENT CHECKS

Prior to commencing the descent, a check should be made to review the fuel tanks selected and their contents. This check fulfils two safety considerations:

- To ensure that when restrictions apply to the use of auxiliary or supplementary tanks, e.g. when limited to use in level flight only, the main tanks are selected before descending.
- To ensure that the tanks selected have sufficient fuel in them and so avoid the need to change tanks during the descent or when the aircraft is at low altitudes.

Additionally the mixture controls will need readjustment and the cowl flaps or cooling gills may have to be partially or fully closed if a prolonged descent is envisaged.

A point to remember in relation to the use of mixture controls during the descent phase is that placing them into the fully rich position at altitude prior to a long descent can lead to fouling of the spark plugs whilst low power settings are being used. Therefore when long descents are planned it may be advisable (depending upon the recommendations in the aircraft manual) to enrich the mixtures progressively during descent.

It is also good practice generally, and specifically in Instrument Meteorological Conditions, to note the altimeter settings, and to re-set these as necessary prior to commencing the descent.

More frequent observation of the cylinder head temperatures should be made whilst descending and the cowl flaps or gills adjusted as necessary to maintain the recommended cylinder head temperatures.

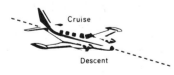

When levelling off from the descent, anticipate the selected cruising altitude and if a low rpm setting has been used, increase this to the required figure before adjusting the manifold pressure.

The operational altitudes of twin engined aircraft are normally higher than those of single engined types, and therefore the cruise descent is often a more economical and sensible procedure, and one which will also ensure greater passenger comfort.

The rate of descent should be selected according to the aircraft's groundspeed and required altitude reduction.

When fairly rapid descents are required, it is sometimes beneficial to lower landing gear and/or flaps to ensure that some power can be maintained to keep the engine temperatures at a reasonable level. In these circumstances care should be exercised prior to, and during, the descent, to ensure the V_{le} and V_{lo} are not exceeded.

When an auto pilot has been used, it would normally be wise to disengage it before or during the descent. The aircraft manual should be consulted for limitation on the use of the auto pilot, especially in relation to the minimum height at which it can be engaged.

EMERGENCY DESCENT

This is essentially a very rapid descent and the procedure for its implementation will usually be outlined in the particular aircraft manual. The reason for conducting this manoeuvre will be the result of a number of variables, from failure of the cabin pressurisation or oxygen system, to weather or other operational considerations.

When carrying out rapid descents of this nature it will be important to ensure that the V_{ra} (maximum speed for flight in rough air) or V_{no} is not exceeded during passage through turbulent layers.

TURNING

Normal turning manoeuvres, including both 30° banked, and rate 1 level, climbing and descending turns, will be practised to allow the student to become familiar with the rate of roll resulting from control pressures, and the amount of control column and rudder pressures required to variously maintain altitude, airspeed, and balance. This practice will also include rolling out of turns onto preselected headings.

SLOW FLIGHT AND STALLING

Prior to stalling practice, the pilot should be introduced to 'slow flight' with the aircraft in different configurations during level, turning, climbing and descending flight. The minimum airspeed selected should not be less than the V_{sse} (when quoted) or alternatively not less than 10 knots above the V_{mc} for the specific aircraft type.

STALLING

The following information concerning stall entries and recoveries is of a general nature and the Flight/Owner's Manual/Pilot's Operating Handbook for the specific aircraft type must be consulted to ensure that any limitations or restrictions with regard to aircraft configuration, power settings and altitudes in relation to stalling practice are complied with.

The stalling demonstrations and practice are similar to those carried out during basic training, but a few additional points will apply:

1. Due to the additional weight of twin engined aircraft and consequent greater height loss during a stall, it is of more importance that an impending stall situation is quickly recognised and recovery effected before an actual stall occurs.

   For this reason most of a pilot's stall training during twin engined conversion must be aimed at early recognition and recovery prior to the developed stall occurring. Less time will therefore be spent on practising recovery from developed stalls.

2. Although the immediate and full application of power is a vital and necessary feature of stall recovery (if a minimum loss of altitude is to be achieved), there is also another very important consideration. This relates to flight in the region of V_{mc}, and can be explained as follows:

   Many twin engined aircraft have stalling speeds which are close to or below V_{mca}. Therefore a partial or complete loss of power from one engine when the throttles are rapidly moved forward during the recovery stage could cause a situation where directional and lateral control is lost, and a spin could easily be induced.

   Due to this possibility, it is important to open the throttles more slowly than is usual in single engined aircraft during stall recovery. This technique will allow a pilot more time to maintain control should temporary power loss, or partial or full power failure, occur to one engine during the initial recovery stage.

3. When practising stalls entered from a climb, the stalling speed will be lower, and therefore because of the reasons given in (2) it will be advisable to use less than normal climbing power during entry.

4. It will often be found that a secondary stall can more easily be induced during the recovery than with single engined aircraft. Caution must therefore be exercised when moving the control column back following the initial part of the recovery procedure.

Safety Checks and Power Selection
The normal safety checks will be carried out, but in addition:

- Fuel tank selection will be of greater importance, i.e. it may be prohibited on some twin engined aircraft to have other than the main tanks selected during stalling practice or other unusual manoeuvres.
- If an auto pilot is fitted it should be checked and set in the 'OFF' position.
- The rpm are normally set for cruise climb power or at the top of the green arcs.
- Due to the greater rate of sink and consequently the greater height loss during the stall, the recommended minimum entry altitude should be higher than that used for stalling practice in single engined aircraft.
- The result of an engine failure occurring during the stall entry and recovery must be borne in mind throughout the stalling practice.

Symptoms of the Stall
The main symptoms are a reduction in noise level (power off or low power stalls), decreasing response from the primary controls, the activation of aural or warning light signals, and on many aircraft there may also be some buffeting.

Recovery With and Without Power
Both types of recovery should be practised and the procedures are the same as for single engined aircraft, apart from the greater time taken to apply full power during those practices requiring the use of the engines.

Recovery When a Wing Drops
The standard recovery procedure in which use of the ailerons is delayed until safely above stalling speed is generally applicable to all types of aircraft. Rudder is used to prevent the further yaw associated with a wing dropping at the point of stall.

Stall Entry With Power On
It will normally be advisable to limit the amount of entry power used during this practice (for reasons already explained). It must also be appreciated that a stall using maximum climbing power will result in a very high nose attitude. Regardless of the amount of power used it will always be advisable to avoid rapid (dynamic) entries, due to the possibility of a wing dropping markedly and rapidly.

Higher power settings for stall entries may be employed when the landing gear and flaps are lowered, as the additional drag in this condition will give a lower attitude in pitch at the stall. Anticipation of a rapid wing drop must nevertheless be maintained.

Stall Entry With Flaps Down
Several stall entries and recoveries should be practised with various stages of flap set. Safety checks prior to these entries must include monitoring the airspeed to ensure that flaps are not lowered whilst still above V_{fe}. Furthermore, the pilot will have to be careful to ensure the V_{fe} is not exceeded during the recovery.

Stalls in the Approach Configuration
These should be practised from straight and turning flight with landing gear down and maximum flap lowered. The standard recovery will apply in all cases.

Recoveries at the Incipient Stage
Due to the additional height loss normally associated with heavier aircraft and the advisability of a slight delay in the rate of applying power, the need for a recovery to be implemented at the incipient stage of the stall will be a paramount consideration during training. Therefore, although it is good practice to investigate the aircraft characteristics up to the developed stall, the major part of a pilot's training in this exercise must be directed towards recovering at the incipient stage.

Recovery During Changes of Configuration
It must be appreciated that a stall situation can develop at any power setting, during any manoeuvre and with the aircraft in any configuration. Additionally it is possible for a stall to occur when the flaps or landing gear are being lowered or raised. It will therefore be useful to practise a few stall entries and recoveries whilst changes in the aircraft configuration are being made.

ADVANCED TURNING

The objective of practising steeply banked turns is for a pilot to develop competence at control and co-ordination in conditions of changing load factors. The bank angles used should be at least 45°.

Maintaining a constant altitude will be a little more difficult in a twin engined aircraft due to the greater airspeed, and the control pressures will need to be more positive in order to stop any tendency to climb or descend.

Without a fuselage mounted engine cowl, the nose of the aircraft usually slopes downwards at a steeper angle. This can result in

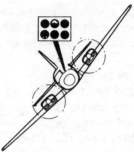

minimal or poor positive visual pitch reference immediately in front
of the pilot. This lack of positive visual reference will result in a
greater need to cross refer to the attitude indicator, and a more
frequent monitoring of the altimeter and VSI.

Steep turns while in level, climbing, or descending flight should be
practised to allow the pilot to appreciate the rate and amount of
control pressure necessary under these flight conditions.

Power will normally have to be increased slightly to maintain the
entry airspeed when level steep turns are being practised. As a
measure of proficiency the airspeed should not vary by more than
10 knots, and the altitude should be maintained within ± 100′ and
the bank angle within 5° during the manoeuvre.

RECOVERY FROM UNUSUAL ATTITUDES

For training purposes these can be divided into:

● A steeply banked, nose high attitude.
● The entry to a power on spiral descent.

Recovery from the near stall situation in a steeply banked turn
with the nose high should be effected by rolling the wings level
smoothly and applying forward pressure to the control column whilst
increasing the power as necessary.

Recovery from the descending spiral type situation is to roll the
wings level firmly whilst reducing power. Care must be used to avoid
a high load factor being applied during recovery from the wings level
dive which follows. Therefore although a positive backward pressure
on the control column will be required, it must be applied smoothly
and gently.

Note: Multi engined aircraft are commonly stressed to lower load
factors than single engined aircraft, and these factors will be
significantly reduced when flaps are in the lowered position. The
specific Flight/Owner's Manual/Pilot's Operating Handbook must be
consulted to establish the maximum load factors which are permitted
with and without flaps lowered, the manoeuvring speed, and also
whether there are any angle of bank limitations.

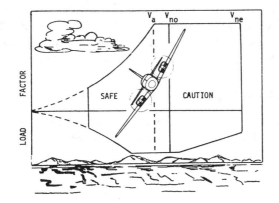

STALLING IN THE TURN

Once again it must be appreciated that high load factors are to be avoided and therefore dynamic entries to the stall, i.e. rapid backward movement of the control column at cruising airspeeds whilst steeply banked, should be avoided.

A useful entry method is to reduce the speed to approximately 1·25 times the stalling speed and re-trim. The turn entry should then be carried out, and whilst maintaining a constant bank of about 40°, increase the back pressure gradually and continuously to induce the stall symptoms. Recovery should be initiated immediately the stall symptoms are recognised.

Recovery is achieved by forward pressure on the control column and as the airspeed increases the wings should be rolled level and power adjusted as necessary.

INSTRUMENT APPRECIATION

At the end of this flight and whilst the aircraft is being flown back to the aerodrome, a short period of instrument appreciation on full panel should be carried out.

An applicant for a multi engine rating who has no instrument qualification will not be required to demonstrate proficiency in all aspects of instrument flight. Nevertheless the ability to retain control during conditions of very poor visibility or inadvertent cloud penetration will be considered an essential part of pilot competence.

Instrument appreciation is therefore a mandatory exercise during multi engine conversion, and this should include all normal flight manoeuvres, and recognition of and recovery from unusual attitudes.

It will be noted that at the higher cruising speeds of twin engined aircraft a greater amount of stability will be experienced. This means a stable instrument flying platform, and as a result firmer control pressures will be required when correcting for attitude changes.

CIRCUIT, APPROACH AND LANDING

A second review of the circuit, approach and landing procedures will be carried out at the concluding stage of this flight.

Part 1   Normal Flight: Sequence 3

Long Briefing

OBJECTIVES

To teach the pilot the normal procedures and techniques used for multi engined aircraft during take-offs, circuits, approaches and landings, and to ensure competence is achieved in these procedures and techniques before proceeding to the asymmetric stage of his flight training.

The following items will be covered in this briefing:

Pre Take-Off Checks
Into Wind Take-Offs
Crosswind Take-Offs
Short/Soft Field Take-Offs
Circuit Procedures
Powered Approaches and Landings
Crosswind Approach and Landing
Short/Soft Field Approaches and Landings
Mislanding and Going Round Again

The procedure for normal and crosswind take-offs, approaches and landings, including the considerations relating to drills and checks, have already been introduced in Sequence 1 of these Long Briefings. This briefing, therefore, should be used to ensure the pilot under training has no queries relating to his previous training, and to cover in greater depth the need for reviewing and complying with certain significant speeds prior to and during the take-off, approach and landing. It will also be used to introduce the techniques applicable to the various types of take-offs, approaches and landings and those which apply in the event of a mislanding or the need to go round again.

SIGNIFICANT SPEEDS USED DURING TAKE-OFF

Most aircraft manuals quote the approximate speed at which the nosewheel should be raised off the ground, and also the speed for 'lift off'. Either prior to or just after lift off (depending upon the aircraft type) a speed known as V_2 will be reached. This is an arbitrary speed which is sufficiently above the V_{mca} to ensure that the pilot could safely control the aircraft in the event of the sudden failure of the critical engine. It is therefore termed 'Safety Speed' or the 'Recommended Safe Single Engined Speed'. V_{mca} has already been covered in the ground training section of this manual, and the pilot must also be fully aware of this speed before take-off.

Once V_2 has been reached, the next important speed to achieve will be the best rate of climb speed on one engine. This is termed V_{yse}, and at or above this speed, the pilot will have the best opportunity to continue to climb should an engine fail.

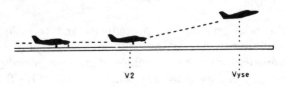

It must nevertheless be remembered that small twin engined aircraft do not necessarily have to demonstrate a climb capability on one engine in order to achieve certification, and the Flight/Owner's Manual/Pilot's Operating Handbook for the particular aircraft must be referred to in order to establish the single engined performance.

Depending upon the type of climb required, i.e. the best rate or best angle of climb, the V_y or V_x should next be established and held, until a safe height or clearance above all obstacles ahead of the aircraft has been achieved.

An additional aspect of take-off performance will be the 'Accelerate–Stop   Distance'.

(Refer to page 82.) This is the distance needed to accelerate to the safety speed, or V_{mca}, and includes, in the event of one engine failing, the additional distance required to bring the aircraft to a stop using heavy braking.

The total distance required will clearly vary with the take-off conditions, e.g. aircraft weight, wind component and the take-off surface. Most aircraft manuals contain graphs or tables from which this distance can be calculated.

THE SHORT FIELD TAKE-OFF

The short field take-off is a procedure which should be carried out when obstruction clearance along the take-off path is considered to be less than that normally acceptable but still safely practicable. It will therefore relate to the take-off distance available, and the airspeed for the best angle of climb should be adopted immediately following take-off. This airspeed should be maintained until a safe clearance above all obstructions is established.

The longest possible take-off run, as directly into wind as is possible, should be used in these circumstances. It can generally be stated that the use of the short field take-off technique at normal aerodromes will be confined to those occasions when the wind is light and the aircraft is at maximum all up weight. However, air temperature, airfield surface, and altitude, will also have a bearing upon the decision to use this procedure.

All the items which have already been learned while flying single engined aircraft will apply, and the Flight/Owner's Manual/Pilot's Operating Handbook must be consulted to determine whether the use of flap is recommended, and also whether the short field technique will safely guarantee clearance from the particular obstructions in the prevailing circumstances.

Note: At lower altitudes some aircraft may have a V_x which is less than V_{mca}, and therefore an engine failure during a climb at the speed for the best angle of climb would result in the aircraft becoming uncontrollable should the engine failure occur when the aircraft was close to the ground. In this event the supplementary recovery procedure will be necessary, i.e. the aircraft nose will have to be lowered quickly and the power reduced on the operating engine.

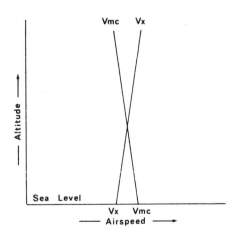

THE SOFT FIELD TAKE-OFF

As for single engined aircraft, the use of flaps during this type of take-off can generally be assumed to offer an advantage, because the stalling speed will be lower, so allowing a reduced lift off speed to be used.

It must nevertheless be appreciated that the use of the soft field technique may negate the principle of achieving a safety speed (when possible) prior to lift off.

In normal circumstances the use of the soft field take-off will be confined to situations which involve soft ground, long grass, snow covered or rough surfaces. Provided the degree of obstruction clearance permits, the safest procedure will therefore be to remain in level flight immediately following lift off, until V_2 or V_{yse} is reached.

Note: When a take-off has been carried out from a snow or slush covered surface, and the air temperature immediately above the surface is at or below 0° C, it will be advisable to delay retraction of the landing gear for a short while. This will allow any snow or slush which may have been thrown up onto the landing gear mechanism to be dried off. If this procedure is not followed it will be possible for the landing gear to become frozen in the retracted position.

Finally, and regardless of the take-off technique used, a further consideration will apply when taking off from surfaces where loose stones or similar debris are present. In these circumstances the pilot must be careful not to use high power when the aircraft is stationary, or damage will occur to the propeller blades.

CIRCUIT PROCEDURES

The climb immediately after take-off should normally be conducted at the best rate of climb speed until a safe height is reached, after which a higher climbing speed may be used. During the initial stages of the climb the landing gear and the flaps (if used) are retracted.

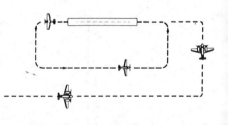

Once circuit height is reached the power settings should be adjusted to give a level flight airspeed below V_{fe} and V_{lo}, and normally the fuel pumps should be left in the 'ON' position when practising circuits and landings. The RTF call is made in the downwind position and the pre-landing checks completed. Power adjustment may have to be made to offset the increased drag when the landing gear is lowered.

Because of the higher cruising speeds, care must be exercised to keep clear of slower aircraft whilst in the circuit, and it is normal to make a slightly wider crosswind leg in order to maintain a safe distance from slower aircraft when downwind. It will also be advisable to increase the length of the downwind leg in order to give more time for adjusting the aircraft position prior to the base leg and final approach.

POWERED APPROACH AND LANDING

The base leg is used to set up the final approach path, and to make the necessary adjustments to flaps and power. The glide approach is not normally used during multi engined aircraft operations.

In the event of failure of one engine at this stage a decision may have to be made to continue the approach or go round again. If it becomes necessary to go round again the decision must be made before reaching a certain minimum height because of performance considerations. This height is known as the 'Asymmetric Committal Height' and it will vary according to the aircraft type, all up weight and other factors, but during training it is generally accepted as 500' agl. The use of asymmetric committal height is explained in more detail in Part 2, Long Briefing Sequence No 3.

Once below this height a critical situation could easily occur if an attempt was made to carry out a go around on one engine. This would arise because of the height loss incurred whilst attempting to establish a climb, and raising the flap and landing gear at a time when the airspeed is low and the ability to accelerate is strictly limited.

USE OF FLAP

Flaps are used in the normal manner, with the final flap selection being made when established on the final approach.

THE FINAL APPROACH AND LANDING

Because of the higher approach airspeeds used, it will be necessary to gradually reduce the speed in the final stages, to arrive at the recommended threshold speed laid down or advised in the aircraft manual. This threshold speed should be increased in turbulent conditions.

Throughout the approach it is important to appreciate that a heavier aircraft will need more time to react to power changes when regulating the rate of descent. The pilot must therefore develop a greater anticipation in relation to an undershoot or overshoot situation.

Anticipation

The degree of actual anticipation needed will vary with the aircraft weight, weather conditions and the terrain (including larger obstructions) in the vicinity of the approach path.

A useful *aide-mémoire* to ensure the landing gear is down and locked is to include in the RTF 'Finals' call the words *three greens*. The question of whether the rpm levers are moved fully forward or left in the high power cruise position is largely a matter of personal choice. Some pilots prefer to place the rpm levers fully forward during the approach in order that full power can immediately be achieved by moving the throttles forward. When this method is used, the pilot should take care to ensure that the manifold pressures are relatively low when moving the rpm levers to the forward position, thus minimising the effects of sudden engine noise to people living in the vicinity of the approach path.

A second method is to leave the rpm at a high cruise setting which then reduces the possibility of temporarily overspeeding the propellers in the event of applying full throttle during a missed approach, or similar situation.

Whilst it is not incorrect to have the rpm levers in the high cruise position during the final stages of the approach, it should be appreciated that if an engine failure occurs, it will normally be necessary to select the maximum rpm position if a 'go around' is needed, and this will be an additional action for the pilot to carry out during what might well be a stress situation.

THE LANDING

Due to the aircraft's greater weight and wing loading, the rate of sink can be appreciable and sudden if the throttles are closed rapidly at low airspeed, and it could result in a heavy landing. Therefore it is advisable to maintain some power until almost to the ground. Then, whilst carrying out the flare, the power should be gradually reduced.

The touchdown should be made on the mainwheels first, and the nosewheel then lowered gently to the ground before elevator effectiveness is lost.

CROSSWIND LANDINGS

These are achieved in the normal manner but because the approach and touchdown speeds are higher, any given crosswind component will have less effect than with a lighter or slower single engined aircraft.

FLAPLESS LANDINGS

Twin engined aircraft require a longer landing distance and landing run, and because of this it is important to place the aircraft accurately as near to the runway threshold as is compatible with safety. The pilot must also be prepared to use firm braking. The recommended speeds for this type of landing must be obtained from the aircraft manual.

SHORT FIELD LANDING

This is accomplished by carrying out a powered approach with full flap being lowered in the final stages. Accurate airspeed and power adjustments should be made to arrive a few feet above the pre-determined touchdown point at the correct airspeed.

Any recommendations in relation to the amount of flap to use in crosswind conditions should be complied with.

SOFT FIELD LANDING

The approach and landing flare is carried out in the same manner as for a short field approach and landing. Unless the landing distance is restricted the point of touchdown is of less importance than the requirement to touchdown at the lowest possible speed.

Note: Short/Soft Field Landings

If flaps are raised immediately after touchdown to improve tyre adhesion and braking (short field landing) or to maintain elevator effectiveness (soft field landing), additional care must be taken to avoid selecting the landing gear lever by mistake.

MISLANDING

Should a mislanding arise at or close to the point of touchdown, it will be inadvisable to attempt to recover from this and continue with the landing. Normally the safest course of action will be to apply take-off power and establish the aircraft safely in the climb. Following this, the landing gear and flaps can be retracted after the situation is under control and a safe airspeed and height have been achieved.

GOING ROUND AGAIN

Immediately the decision is made to carry out 'go round again' action, the throttles should be advanced to maximum power but care should be taken to avoid exceeding the manifold pressure and rpm limitations.

The landing gear should be raised at this point and if flaps have been selected these should be retracted in stages to avoid sudden attitude change in pitch and to guard against the possibility of a sudden sink occurring. If full flap were to be raised in one stage, particularly if the airspeed were low, a rapid rate of sink might occur.

When these actions have been completed the aircraft should be established in the normal climb and re-positioned in the circuit pattern. Consideration must be given to the advisability of climbing to one side of the runway in order to keep in sight any aircraft which may be taking off.

When carrying out 'touch and go' landings the flaps should normally be left down until the aircraft is safely airborne, as this avoids the possibility of an inadvertent 'wheels up' selection whilst the aircraft is still rolling along the ground. However, in the case of those aircraft which have a 'wheelbarrowing' tendency it may be advisable to raise the flaps partially prior to increasing the power, or in any event before the aircraft is airborne.

Note: Some landing gear and flap systems are interconnected in such a way that the landing gear 'warning horn' will sound if the gear is unlocked whilst the flaps are set at more than 15°. When an interconnected system of this type is fitted it will usually be advisable to select flaps to 15° immediately following the attainment of a suitable airspeed, after the application of power, and prior to selecting the landing gear up. Thus, pilot distractions resulting from the landing gear horn sounding following application of take-off power and selection of wheels up will be avoided.

Part 2   Asymmetric Flight: Sequence 1

Long Briefing

OBJECTIVES

To teach the student how to recognise the failure of one engine during flight, and to control the aircraft safely in varying conditions of asymmetric flight at normal operating altitudes.

The following items will be covered during this briefing:

Introduction to Asymmetric Flight
Effects and Recognition of Engine Failure in Level Flight
Methods of Control and Identification of the Failed Engine
Effects and Recognition of Engine Failure During Turns
Effects of Varying Speed and Power

Due to the many variations which occur between multi engined aircraft, their systems, and the operation of such systems, these briefing notes cannot cater for individual types of aircraft. They are therefore confined to a systematic coverage of the general points in flight on asymmetric power.

INTRODUCTION TO ASYMMETRIC FLIGHT

This will consist of feathering a propeller and shutting down one engine at a safe altitude to demonstrate that the aircraft can be safely operated on one engine during level, turning and descending flight.

A single engine climb will also be performed to demonstrate the reduced performance when one engine is inoperative.

It will also need to be appreciated that during single engined flight a significantly higher power setting on the operating engine will be necessary and therefore the oil temperature and pressure gauges, and cylinder head temperature gauges, must be monitored more frequently. Care must also be exercised with regard to the mixture control, and this should be moved to a richer position if the cylinder head temperature on the operating engine rises beyond that which is normally recommended.

This demonstration will in the interests of safety normally be conducted above 3000′ agl so that in the event of abnormal operation of the operating engine occurring, time will be available to restart the engine which has been shut down.

During most of a student's practice in asymmetric flight it will be inconvenient, and at low altitudes unsafe, to feather a propeller. Therefore, instead of feathering, a power setting known as *Zero Thrust* will be used to simulate the actual drag reduction experienced when a propeller is feathered. This zero thrust power is normally shown in aircraft manuals in graph form, which usually allows for the effects of altitude and temperature.

When a 'zero thrust' graph is not incorporated in the aircraft manual, an approximate zero thrust setting can be determined in flight by selecting an airspeed suitable for level flight on one engine. This should be established with the critical engine feathered, and the other engine operating at a high cruise rpm, with the foot load trimmed out. The critical engine should then be unfeathered and the manifold pressure adjusted to give the same airspeed as when it was feathered, with the aeroplane still trimmed for balanced flight. This manifold pressure can then be used as the zero thrust setting for later asymmetrc practice.

It should nevertheless be noted that a setting obtained in this way can only be approximate due to variations in altitude and temperature. However, the use of this zero thrust setting will produce a similar foot load on the appropriate rudder pedal to that experienced by the pilot when an engine is feathered.

EFFECTS AND RECOGNITION OF ENGINE FAILURE DURING STRAIGHT AND LEVEL FLIGHT

The aircraft will be set up in normal straight and level flight at cruising power, and one throttle slowly closed so that the resulting motions of yaw, roll and a spiral descent are each clearly demonstrated. The aircraft will then be returned to normal two engined straight and level flight, and the other engine throttled back to demonstrate the same effects.

METHODS OF CONTROL AND IDENTIFICATION OF THE FAILED ENGINE

The unbalance of the thrust and drag forces and the effects of the subsequent yaw have already been covered in the Ground Syllabus section of this manual. Nevertheless, it is of value at this point to reiterate the importance of using sufficient rudder to prevent yaw whilst using the ailerons in the normal way to maintain lateral level.

It is particularly important not to use a combination of too little rudder and too much aileron, because the turn and balance indicator will not give a positive indication of the approach to a critical directional control situation at lower airspeeds. Additionally, the use of too much aileron regardless of speed may accentuate yaw as a result of the larger deflections of the ailerons.

The demonstration will be made by closing one throttle whilst using the rudder and ailerons to maintain a constant heading with the wings level. The power of the operating engine will usually need to be increased and the aircraft attitude in pitch adjusted in order to maintain a constant altitude at a safe airspeed.

SUPPLEMENTARY CONTROL OF YAW

Should an engine fail when the aircraft is flying at an airspeed lower than V_{mc} it will be impossible to control the yaw by use of rudder alone. In these circumstances it will be necessary to lower the aircraft nose to increase speed, and reduce power on the operating engine as necessary until control is regained.

This action will need to be done immediately and smoothly to avoid serious loss of control in the form of a rapid yaw, roll and spin entry. Should a spin develop, the throttles should be closed completely and normal spin recovery attempted (subject to any specific directions contained in the aircraft manual).

The supplementary recovery will also need to be used when the airspeed is above V_{mc} should the airspeed be falling rapidly, e.g. a high nose up attitude with high power on the operating engine.

IDENTIFICATION OF THE INOPERATIVE ENGINE

The next stage of flight training concerns the development of ability to quickly determine which engine has failed. When flying a conventional twin engined aircraft the pilot will sense the asymmetric thrust which occurs through the effect of yaw and roll towards the failed engine.

As the aircraft commences to yaw, rudder pressure must be applied to maintain directional control, therefore the 'working foot' is on the same side as the working engine. However, after an engine failure the pilot's immediate and follow up procedures will be concerned  primarily with the failed engine and therefore as an aid to identification of the inoperative engine it is preferable to think in terms of '*Idle Foot – Idle Engine*'. For example, if a pilot's right foot is not applying rudder pressure, then the right engine is the one that has failed.

Use of Engine Instruments for Identification of the Failed Engine

When the aircraft is being flown at cruising or higher power, the yaw produced from an engine failure is sufficient to enable a pilot to identify which engine has failed. However, when an aircraft is being operated at low power, e.g. the descent phase, there is the possibility that the small yaw force, resulting from a low power setting on the functioning engine, may go unnoticed for a period of time. Therefore when in this flight phase the pilot will need to be alert for any indications from his engine instruments that an engine failure has occurred.

Identification of engine failure which may be obtained from the engine instruments will vary with types of instruments used in a particular aircraft, and also with the engine power being used at the time. Therefore the information given in this manual is of a general nature only.

On some aircraft, and depending upon the power setting, the tachometer will show a significant drop of 200 rpm or more, and on others there may be no indications from this source. This latter is due to the ability of some types of CSU to maintain a constant rpm over a wider range of manifold pressure.

When fuel flowmeters are fitted, these will usually give an immediate indication of engine failure, but fuel pressure gauges will not be a reliable source of information unless the engine failure is due to fuel starvation.

When exhaust gas temperature analysers are fitted, these will give a rapid indication of temperature drop and are therefore useful in confirming the identification of which engine has failed. Cylinder head temperature readings will also give a positive indication of which engine has failed, but the change in engine temperature will take place over a longer period.

From the above information it will be seen that engine instrument indications can be of value in confirming which engine has failed, but are of less use for the purpose of making a rapid identification.

Confirmation of Identification

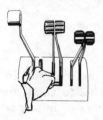

Once the initial identification of the failed engine has been made, it should be confirmed by gradually closing the throttle of that engine. If no reduction in noise level or change in foot load occurs, the pilot's identification has been positively confirmed, and he can then proceed to implement the procedures necessary to establish the reason for failure.

Note: When only partial engine failure has occurred, closing the throttle of the correct engine will create the need for an increased pressure on the appropriate rudder pedal.

Visual and Flight Instrument Indications
When using cruising or climbing power during visual flight conditions, the yaw and roll produced from the asymmetric power and drag will be clearly seen through outside visual references.

On those occasions when flight is being conducted in very poor visibility or in cloud, the turn and balance indicators will clearly show an abnormal situation, in that the balance ball will move *'towards the operating engine'* and the Attitude and Turn Indicators will show a *'roll and turn towards the inoperative engine'*. The displacement of the ball or other balance indicator is, however, the primary indication as it is this which distinguishes between a turn caused by engine failure and one due to other causes.

In turbulent weather, particularly during a descent at low power, the indications from the flight instruments will not be so readily interpreted and the pilot will need to be extra alert on such occasions.

EFFECTS AND RECOGNITION OF ENGINE FAILURE DURING TURNS

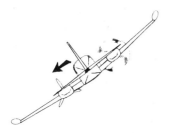

Recognition of an engine failure during climbing or level turns is normally straightforward, as the aircraft will yaw and roll towards the inoperative engine regardless of whether it is being flown in a laterally level or banked attitude.

EFFECT OF 'INSIDE' ENGINE FAILURE
If during a turn the inside engine fails, e.g. the left engine during a left turn, the roll will be pronounced and a spiral dive condition with a marked loss of altitude will occur if no corrective action is taken.

EFFECT OF 'OUTSIDE' ENGINE FAILURE
If the outside engine fails during a turn, e.g. the right engine during a left turn, the aircraft will yaw and roll away from the direction of turn and control of this situation is more easily achieved.

POSSIBILITY OF CONFUSION IN IDENTIFICATION DURING TURNING FLIGHT
During a turn it is possible for a pilot to experience greater difficulty in identifying the failed engine, because the aeroplane may already

be out of balance and the angle of bank may be changing for other reasons at the moment of engine failure.

If any doubt exists as to which engine has failed, the best immediate procedure is to return to laterally level flight and identify the failed engine from this flight condition.

Having made this statement, it should nevertheless be appreciated that multi engined aircraft can be fully controlled in the event of engine failure during turns involving steep bank angles, but performance in respect of the maintenance of altitude and airspeed will be significantly impaired.

VISUAL AND FLIGHT INSTRUMENT INDICATIONS

The comments previously made in relation to visual and instrument indications of engine failure during normal level flight will also apply when the aircraft is turning, although on some aircraft the balance ball will tend to 'hunt' between the neutral position and an out of balance position until control is regained.

EFFECT OF VARYING AIRSPEED AND POWER

The relationship between airspeed and thrust in asymmetric flight is such that the higher the airspeed, the greater will be the effective force which can be provided by the rudder to counteract yaw. Additionally a smaller movement of the ailerons will be required to maintain the wings laterally level. On the other hand, for a given airspeed, the greater the thrust from the operating engine, the greater will be the asymmetric yaw and roll.

AT NORMAL CRUISING AIRSPEED AND POWER

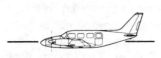

The flight demonstration to show this effect will commence at a selected airspeed and power setting in straight and level trimmed flight. One throttle will then be closed whilst preventing yaw with rudder, maintaining lateral level with the ailerons, and altitude with the elevators. The airspeed will then settle at a new and lower figure.

Once the new airspeed is established, the nose of the aircraft will be raised and the airspeed reduced to approximately V_{yse}. At this lower airspeed more rudder

Vyse

will be required to maintain the aircraft on a constant heading and in balance.

Coarser use of the ailerons will also be needed to keep the wings laterally level. From this it will be positively seen that at lower airspeeds larger control movements will be necessary to maintain control of the aircraft.

AT LOW SAFE AIRSPEED AND CLIMBING POWER

Whilst maintaining the V_{yse} the power will be increased on the operating engine and it will be noted that a significantly larger rudder deflection, together with an increased foot load, will be needed to maintain heading and balance, and even coarser use of ailerons will be required to keep the wings laterally level.

From these two demonstrations it will be appreciated that when maintaining control of the aircraft in asymmetric flight, the largest deflection of the controls will occur when the power is high and the airspeed is low, and thus this is the most demanding case in terms of regaining and maintaining control.

AT HIGH AIRSPEED AND LOW POWER

This demonstration will commence by setting up a descent at cruising airspeed and low power. Once the aircraft is trimmed and established in the descent, the power on one engine will be further reduced to simulate partial power failure.

The small asymmetric yaw and roll effect can then be noted, enabling an appreciation of the possibility of failing to recognise partial power loss from one engine in this situation.

The selected throttle will now be further closed until it is in the idle position, demonstrating that even when total power failure of one engine occurs in this type of descent, the visual and instrument indications of engine failure might go unnoticed, particularly in turbulent weather conditions.

AIRMANSHIP (ALL SEQUENCES)

During the asymmetric stage of training, special emphasis must be placed upon determining the circumstances when actual feathering practice may be undertaken, e.g. at sufficient altitude, and when at a relatively short distance from an aerodrome.

Care will be necessary to ensure that misunderstandings are avoided in relation to which engine is to be shut down. This will also require a clear agreement between instructor and student as to who is responsible for operating the associated systems and services in the cockpit.

It is often wise to associate positively, e.g. by the words 'Left or Right', in relation to the engine it is intended to affect before moving the controls to be used.

On those occasions when practice procedures do not involve an engine being feathered and shut down, the use of accurate *'Touch Drills'* will be required. Such occasions will also need a clear agreement between instructor and student as to the manner in which the touch drills are to be made as well as the fact that the propeller is not actually to be feathered.

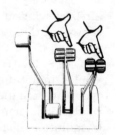

During those periods when one engine is shut down or operating at zero thrust, it is particularly important to monitor the operating engine's oil and cylinder head temperatures, oil pressure, fuel flow, and associated services at frequent intervals.

It will also be necessary to monitor the temperatures of the inoperative engine, not only so that the appropriate re-starting and warming up action may be taken but also to be aware that adequate safe power may not be readily available from a cold engine should it be needed rapidly, e.g. in the event of malfunction of the operating engine.

The above airmanship points are absolutely vital to safety if the aircraft is being flown at low altitude, as there will be little or no time available to rectify a mistake in this situation.

Part 2   Asymmetric Flight: Sequence 2

Long Briefing

OBJECTIVES

To give the student an understanding of, and practice in, controlling the aircraft at the Minimum Control Speed, and to practise the procedures to be adopted in the event of 'In Flight' engine failure. Additionally, to ensure the student has a complete understanding of the effect of engine failure upon aircraft performance.

The following items will be covered during this briefing:

Minimum Control Speeds (V_{mc})
Effect of Bank Angle upon V_{mc}
Effect of Propeller Feathering upon V_{mc}
Effect of the Take-Off Configuration upon V_{mc}
Feathering and Unfeathering Procedures
Engine Failure Procedures
Control and Performance During the Take-Off and Approach Phases
Significance of Safety Speed (V_2)
Significance of Asymmetric Committal Height

Due to the many variations which occur between multi engined aircraft, their systems, and the operation of such systems, these briefing notes cannot cater for individual types of aircraft. They are therefore confined to a systematic coverage of the general points concerning the above items.

MINIMUM CONTROL SPEEDS

The term V_{mc} refers to the minimum speed at which directional control of the aircraft can be maintained with one engine inoperative. Since the ability to retain directional control is related to the amount of yaw produced from the operating engine, the actual value of V_{mc} will vary for any particular aircraft according to the asymmetric thrust and drag produced at various power settings. An aircraft will therefore have a wide range of V_{mc} values (pages 50–59 of the Technical Subjects section refers).

The purpose of demonstrating Minimum Control Speed in flight is to commence a gradual introduction to the control of the aircraft under asymmetric power in critical situations, and is not therefore a demonstration of the aircraft's specified V_{mca}.

In each demonstration the recovery to controlled flight will be initiated either immediately directional control can no longer be maintained, i.e. when the balance ball is significantly displaced from the centre, or when a safe margin above the stall remains. At no stage should the aircraft be allowed to decelerate to a lower airspeed.

On those aircraft where the stalling speed is higher than the minimum control speed in the configuration and power setting being used, it will not be possible to carry out a practical demonstration of V_{mc}.

In those cases where the stalling speed and minimum control speed are very close, extreme care will be needed to avoid a critical situation developing, and in the region of the V_{mc}, the operating engine should be throttled back, whilst the nose is being lowered to increase the airspeed, i.e. use of the supplementary recovery procedure.

ASI COLOUR CODING

Later models of multi engined aircraft are equipped with air speed indicators showing coloured radial lines which indicate significant speeds related to single engined flight.

The best single engine rate of climb speed (V_{yse}) is normally indicated by a blue radial line, and a red radial line is used to indicate the minimum control speed in the take-off configuration. If the aircraft being used does not have this form of colour coding it will be extremely important to review the V_{mca} for the specific aircraft type immediately prior to take-off.

Note: Safety Speed is not indicated by this colour coding method.

DEMONSTRATION OF MINIMUM CONTROL SPEED

This exercise will have to be conducted at a safe altitude, normally not below 2000' agl, therefore when determining the V_{mc} in aircraft with normally aspirated engines it must be appreciated that this airspeed will be slightly lower than the actual V_{mca} due to the reduced density with altitude causing a reduction of the power available from the operating engine.

From a condition of straight and level flight the aircraft will be placed in the climbing attitude (at approximately V_{yse}) and maximum permitted rpm and manifold pressure applied. At this stage one throttle will be gradually closed whilst heading is maintained and the wings kept level.

The aircraft nose will then be raised and the airspeed further reduced. The minimum speed at which directional control can be maintained with the wings level should be noted. This is the minimum control speed for this flight condition. At the point where directional control can no longer be maintained, the nose should be lowered and if necessary the power from the operating engine can be decreased to re-establish control more quickly.

Note: If the particular aircraft's stalling speed in the clean configuration is greater than the minimum control speed it will not be possible to demonstrate the V_{mc}. In these circumstances the use of flap may reduce the stalling speed sufficiently for the demonstration to be effective.

ESTABLISHING THE CRITICAL ENGINE

At the same altitude, repeat the above demonstration closing the opposite throttle, and noting the difference in the minimum control speed obtained. The engine which was throttled back when the higher minimum control speed was obtained is the critical engine. This difference in V_{mc} is normally quite small and may be difficult to detect unless flying in calm air conditions.

Note: If the aircraft is equipped with propellers which rotate in opposite directions, both minimum control speeds will normally be the same, as there will be no critical engine.

EFFECT OF BANK ANGLE UPON V_{mc}

Having found the minimum control speed(s) for the aircraft type in a given configuration, the next step is to determine the effect of V_{mc} of using 5° of bank towards the operating engine.

Using the asymmetric condition which gave the higher V_{mc} (if any), slowly reduce the speed and adopt 5° of bank towards the operating engine before V_{mc} is reached. Note the reduction in minimum control speed.

From this demonstration an appreciation can be obtained of the benefits of a small angle of bank whilst controlling the aircraft in a critical situation, e.g. sudden engine failure at low airspeed near the ground.

EFFECT OF PROPELLER FEATHERING UPON V_{mc}

This will be shown by setting up an asymmetric flight condition similar to the previous demonstrations but with zero thrust set on the critical engine to simulate the effect of feathering.

In this condition the V_{mc} will be less than that previously obtained, thus establishing the importance of feathering the propeller of an inoperative engine as soon as possible when the aircraft is close to the ground.

EFFECT OF THE TAKE-OFF CONFIGURATION UPON V_{mc}

From level flight at a safe altitude the manifold pressure will be reduced, the rpm levers moved fully forward, and the landing gear and take-off flap lowered.

Further reduce power as necessary and adopt the Safety Speed or V_{sse} (whichever is the higher). When no Safety Speed or V_{sse} are quoted in the aircraft manual a speed of at least $V_{mca} \times 1.1$ should be used.

At this stage both throttles will be opened and maximum permitted power selected, following which the throttle of the critical engine will be closed whilst maintaining Safety Speed or its selected equivalent. The airspeed will now be gradually reduced by raising the aircraft's nose and the minimum control speed for this configuration established.

Note: On low powered aircraft operating in turbulent conditions the effect of the take-off configuration upon the V_{mc} may be small and not clearly apparent. Therefore very smooth and accurate handling will be necessary in order to detect the small variation which occurs.

FEATHERING AND UNFEATHERING PROCEDURES

The minimum altitude for the practice of feathering drills is at least 3000′ agl. The actual drills used will be particular to the aircraft type and cannot therefore be covered here. Nevertheless some general points on practice feathering operations can be mentioned as follows:

- Avoid practice feathering during flight in very cold temperatures.
- Limit the engine shut down time to a minimum, close the cowl flap on the feathered engine and ensure the electric fuel pump is off.
- During flight with one engine feathered, monitor the operating engine temperatures frequently.
- During the unfeathering avoid a strong surge in rpm. After

starting, set the pitch lever at a low rpm and the manifold pressure at approximately 15 inches until the engine has warmed up.
● Carefully observe all 'after starting checks' relative to the engine concerned.

ENGINE FAILURE PROCEDURES

Once the maintenance of control has been achieved, the order in which the procedures are carried out will be determined by the phase of flight operation and the aircraft type.

There are two specific flight phases:

(1) Flight at altitude
(2) Flight near the ground

In the case of (1), sufficient time will normally be available for the pilot to carefully check for possible causes of engine failure and when possible rectify the engine malfunction.

In the case of (2) time will be at a premium and the situation could be critical, e.g. if the engine failure occurs during the take-off, approach to landing, or during a 'go around'. It is unlikely that time will permit anything else but controlling the aircraft, determining the engine which has failed, implementing the feathering procedure and in the case of the initial climb out, or during a go round again procedure, establishing the V_{yse}.

In relation to the procedures to be followed it can be stated that variations will inevitably occur between different types of aircraft as to the order and content of the drills and checks which should be implemented. This also extends to different models of the same type, and the procedures detailed in the particular Flight/Owner's Manual/Pilot's Operating Handbook must be carefully studied during conversion training, and at regular intervals afterwards.

Two typical examples of why differences in procedures occur are outlined below:

Example 1. One manual may call for the raising of flaps and landing gear prior to feathering, whilst another may recommend feathering as a first step. The reason for the latter procedure could be due to the fact that some engines cannot be feathered if the rpm drops below a certain figure.

Example 2. In some aircraft, the raising of the landing gear may create more drag during retraction due to the transient position of the landing gear doors, and as a result this action would best be left until feathering has been accomplished and propeller drag reduced.

Therefore the order in which the drills and checks are shown in this manual under 'Immediate' and 'Subsequent' actions must be a general guide only, and the exact order or procedure must be determined by reference to the particular aircraft manual.

However, when engine failure occurs with full flap extended, e.g. a go around from a very low height, the removal of the drag flap should normally be considered to be as important as Feathering.

SIMULATED ENGINE FAILURE PROCEDURES

Although simulated engine failure procedures are normally contained in the particular aircraft manual, the following points should also be borne in mind when carrying out these procedures:

- Avoid closing the throttle abruptly to simulate engine failure. At safe altitudes it will be in the interests of good engine handling to move the mixture control to 'idle cut off' to simulate failure, and after the throttle has been closed to the zero thrust position, the mixture lever should be returned to the rich position.
- Close the cowl flaps on the engine which has been set to zero thrust.
- Frequently monitor the temperatures and oil pressures of both engines.
- When simulated engine failure practice is completed, gradually increase the power on the engine which has been set to zero thrust, and allow it to warm up before selecting normal power.

Note: Whenever simulated engine failure procedures are being practised, there will be occasions when 'Touch Drills' will be employed. This is because there will be circumstances during training in which the safety of the aircraft may be jeopardised if part or all of the procedures concerned were physically carried out, e.g. simulated engine failure near the ground. The occasions where 'Point and Touch' procedures are to be used should be clearly established by the instructor prior to student practice.

ACTUAL ENGINE FAILURE PROCEDURES

In general the following outline of procedures to be implemented after an actual engine failure is self explanatory, and because they must be related to the aircraft type no attempt is made to enter into a detailed account of each action.

In-Flight Engine Failure

In cruise or other flight phases (not including take-off or landing)
- Immediate Actions:
  Maintaining control, including airspeed and use of power
  Recognition of asymmetric condition

Identification and confirmation of the failed engine, Idle Leg – Idle
Engine, and closing of the throttle for confirmation

Cause and Fire Check:

> If an obvious mechanical failure or fire has occurred the
> propeller should be feathered as soon as possible, bearing in
> mind the need to balance a quick reaction against the danger
> of a too hasty reaction which may lead to feathering the
> wrong propeller.

> If no obvious mechanical failure or fire has occurred a
> systematic check should be made to determine the cause of
> failure.

> If the cause of engine failure cannot be rectified the engine
> should be shut down and feathered.

> Drag should be reduced to a minimum and the aircraft
> re-trimmed.

● Subsequent Actions:

Live engine:

> Temperatures, pressures and power setting
> Remaining services available
> Electrical load – assess and reduce as necessary
> Effects on the power source of instruments, landing gear,
> flaps and other services

Final Trimming

Re-Plan Flight – Considerations:

> Review the actions to be completed in relation to:
>> Air Traffic Control services and weather
>> Terrain clearance
>> Action to be taken if unable to maintain altitude
>> Single engined ceiling:
>>> Range and endurance, single engined cruise airspeed
>> Decision to divert or continue along planned route
>> Fuel management:
>>> Best use of remaining fuel
>>> Operation of cross feed (when advisable)
>> The dangers of re-starting a damaged engine
>> Effects on aircraft performance:
>>> Effect on power available and power required
>>> Effect of airframe configuration
> Use of Flight/Owner's Manual/Pilot's Operating Handbook

Airspeeds and Techniques:

> Cruising airspeed (single engine)
> Climbing, ASI colour coding (blue line)
> Descending
> Operating engine – limitations and handling

CONTROL AND PERFORMANCE DURING THE TAKE-OFF OR APPROACH PHASES

Prior to practising engine failure procedure during the take-off and approach phases, a short period involving demonstration and practice at a safe altitude will be given. This will enable the student to appreciate more clearly the problems involved before being asked to practise critical situations near the ground.

SIGNIFICANCE OF TAKE-OFF SAFETY SPEED

Take-off Safety Speed has already been discussed on pages 55–7, and further comments are made in some detail during Long Briefing, Sequence 3 of Part 2 of this manual.

At a safe altitude (minimum 1500′ agl) and away from the circuit area, the aircraft will be set up in trimmed straight and level flight. The airspeed will then be reduced, and the landing gear and take-off flap lowered. The rpm will be set at the maximum permitted and the throttles opened to take-off power. At this stage the airspeed will be reduced to Safety Speed or V_{sse}, whichever is the higher. If no Safety Speed or V_{sse} is quoted in the aircraft manual, a minimum airspeed of at least the $V_{mca} \times 1 \cdot 1$ should be used.

Once the aircraft is established at this airspeed the throttle of the critical engine (if applicable) will be closed to simulate engine failure, and it will be noted that at this airspeed, the ability to maintain directional control is retained.

At this stage the landing gear and flap will be retracted, zero thrust set on the idling engine and V_{yse} adopted. Although the ability to climb on one engine at this altitude may be marginal on some light twin engined aeroplanes, it will be seen that the need to obtain a safe speed prior to lift off is extremely important in relation to aircraft control and performance.

An engine failure at Safety Speed will therefore give the pilot a better opportunity to clean up the aircraft, feather the failed engine, accelerate to V_{yse} and establish a positive rate of climb, whereas an engine failure below this speed will be much more likely to give rise to a hazardous situation.

SIGNIFICANCE OF ASYMMETRIC COMMITTAL HEIGHT

This exercise, like the previous one, will initially be conducted at a safe altitude away from the circuit. It is demonstrated to enable the student to appreciate the need to establish and conform to a self imposed minimum height restriction in the event of being faced with the decision to go round again when the combination of height, airspeed, configuration and power is approaching its most adverse.

The demonstration and practice will consist of setting up a descent in the approach configuration on one engine, with zero thrust and an airspeed equal to V_2 (or its equivalent).

At a nominated height the missed approach procedure will be initiated by applying full power on the operating engine and raising the landing gear and flap. The height loss incurred whilst achieving V_{yse} and establishing a positive rate of climb should be noted.

From the height loss involved it will become clear that no attempt should be made to carry out a missed approach once below a nominated height on the approach when the airspeed is less than V_2 and the aircraft needs to be cleaned up in order that it can climb away. This nominated height is known as the Asymmetric Committal Height and should be considered as that point on any approach below which the pilot must commit himself to a landing should an engine fail. It is thus the equivalent of V_2 in the take-off case.

It will also be advisable to maintain at least V_{yse} during the approach phase until reaching the asymmetric committal height, thus reducing the height loss which would otherwise occur whilst lowering the aircraft nose to achieve the best rate of climb speed on one engine, whenever a missed approach procedure is initiated (see Fig 34).

Fig 34

Note: The nominated height will depend upon the prevailing circumstances.

Part 2   Asymmetric Flight Sequence 3

Long Briefing

OBJECTIVES

To give the student an understanding of the problems involved if an engine fails during the take-off run or shortly after take-off, and to give him practice in controlling the aircraft and applying the procedures necessary to carry out a single engined circuit, approach and landing safely.

The following items will be covered during this briefing:

> Engine Failure During Take-Off
> Engine Failure After Take-Off
> Circuit, Approach and Landing on Asymmetric Power
> Engine Failure During an All Engines Approach or Missed Approach

Due to their importance, certain aspects of asymmetric control and performance which have already been covered in the Technical Subjects section of this manual are repeated during this briefing.

To the pilot the most important minimum control speed will normally be the one which applies should an engine fail during the take-off phase. For this reason a particular speed is quoted in the aircraft manual and termed 'V_{mca}'. It is sometimes referred to as the 'Air Minimum Control Speed'. This speed will most probably have been determined using 5° of bank towards the operating engine.

V_{mca} is established by the aircraft manufacturer to the satisfaction of the airworthiness authorities under specified test conditions, which include a gradual reduction of speed under steady asymmetric power. For certification purposes it is primarily concerned with controllability and indirectly with performance. It defines in effect the ultimate boundary of controllability achievable with forethought and skill.

The technique employed to establish V_{mca} does not take account of the element of surprise, and with the aircraft in this flight condition, a small handling error could result in serious consequences. Therefore engine failure should not be simulated at V_{mca}, because a pilot will normally be unable to control the aircraft safely at this speed, during critical or adverse circumstances, such as near the ground.

Therefore the take-off Safety Speed (V_2) provides a better safety margin, and allows the average pilot more leeway if he decides to continue the take-off or initiate a 'go around' when necessary, assuming normal competence and provided the necessary emergency drills and procedures are completed swiftly but without haste. It is thus the speed applicable to the category of aircraft being discussed in this manual upon which a decision to re-land, forced land, or go round again is based. It is therefore a decision speed.

In high performance multi engined aircraft such as large airliners, Decision Speed is achieved during the take-off run whilst the aeroplane is on the ground, and is known as V_1. This V term is not applicable to light twin engined aircraft certificated in Performance Groups C, D or E, but only to aeroplanes certificated in Performance Group A.

V_2 may also be known as the '50' speed' for certification and operational purposes. The reason for this is that this speed is used in the aircraft certification calculations when determining the take-off and landing distances during operations on asymmetric power. Therefore V_2 has a bearing on climb out and landing performance and will, in fact, be not less than the greater of either 1·1 times V_{mca} or 1·2 times the stalling speed at the take-off weight and configuration. It will in consequence be a variable figure, but in practice on most light twins, a constant figure can be selected and used for controllability purposes.

V_2 may not always be quoted as such in the aeroplane manual, and if this is the case the pilot should check the Performance Section of the manual and use the 50' figure which can normally be found there. If this is not available either, the CAA Airworthiness Division should be asked for guidance.

In some aircraft manuals, pilots will find reference to V_{sse}. This is a specified minimum speed which, if adhered to during actual flight with asymmetric power, including demonstrations of asymmetric performance, will preclude inadvertent entry into the stall/spin regime. However, the term should not be confused with V_2 or Safety Speed.

Furthermore, a pilot may have heard of a number of other V terms concerned with asymmetric power flight which do not apply to light twin engined aircraft, the use of which is not only irrelevant but also confusing. For example, V_1 (Take-Off Decision Speed) and V_{mcl}

(Minimum Control Speed for Landing) are sometimes improperly used in the context of small General Aviation aircraft.

Therefore in the interests of maximum simplicity and clarity compatible with the safe handling of the type of aeroplane to which this manual refers, the pilot need only concern himself with five speeds in relation to asymmetric flight, namely V_{mca}, V_2, V_{yse}, V_{xse} and V_{sse}, the correct use of which should provide him with the protection he needs.

The Pilot's Operating Handbooks which are now replacing the earlier Owner's Manuals clearly state the V_{mca}; however, many Owner's Manuals use the terminology V_{mc} or Minimum Control Speed, and where this occurs it usually relates to the V_{mc} in the take-off configuration.

A further point to bear in mind is that, although for certification purposes the V_{mca} is determined with the most rearward allowable centre of gravity and therefore when the shortest rudder arm applies, pilots are strongly advised against assuming that they can safely use a lower V_{mca} when operating with a forward centre of gravity. Any reduction in minimum control speed due to a forward centre of gravity will be extremely small compared to the dangers of mishandling an engine failure situation during take-off.

ENGINE FAILURE DURING TAKE-OFF

1. Below V_{mca}:
    The two situations to be considered under this heading are:
    (a) When an engine fails below V_{mca}.
    (b) When an engine fails above V_{mca} but before Safety Speed is reached.
    If an engine should fail at any time before reaching V_{mca} the throttles should be closed and the aircraft brought to a stop.

    Prior use of the aircraft manual to determine the accelerate–stop distance in the prevailing conditions will give the pilot a good indication of whether he will be able to stop the aircraft before the end of the runway, or runway and stopway combined.

    If it is known that it will be impossible to stop within the remaining distance available after the throttles are closed, emergency drills such as moving the mixture levers to 'Idle Cut-Off', and turning off fuel switches, etc., should be rapidly accomplished whilst retaining directional control of the aircraft.

    During training, engine failure during the take-off run may be demonstrated provided the distance available in which to stop is clearly sufficient and the surface is good. Liaison with ATC will be an important airmanship feature in this exercise, and in any case it should only be done when other aircraft will not be inconvenienced.

Engine failure between lift off speed and Safety Speed will not be demonstrated and any specific points regarding this type of emergency in relation to the particular aircraft being used should be covered by discussion (see below).

2. Above V_{mca} and Below Safety Speed
During a take-off the most critical time for an engine to fail is during the few seconds when the aircraft is accelerating through the V_{mca} up towards Safety Speed. It is during this period that a wrong decision to continue the take-off or abort will produce an extremely hazardous situation, involving both the aircraft and its occupants.

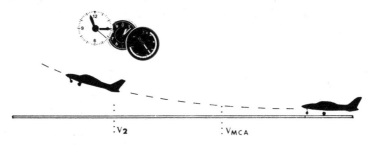

The important considerations which apply to a situation in which the pilot elects to continue the take-off when an engine fails before or even immediately after reaching Safety Speed, are:

● Whether total or partial power failure has occurred, and the amount of power still available
● Aircraft weight, aerodrome, altitude and temperature
● Aircraft configuration – landing gear and flap position
● Length of runway remaining and whether obstructions exist at the aerodrome boundary and in the region of the climb out path

Any attempt to consider this number of variables during a situation in which minimum time and maximum stress apply may easily lead to an incorrect and therefore disastrous decision. Because of this, the pilot should plan to deal with such a contingency prior to the commencement of any take-off.

Bearing in mind the facts already covered in this manual as they relate to V_{mca} and Safety Speed, it can be seen that the most sensible course of action when an engine fails whilst the aircraft is on the ground below Safety Speed is to close both throttles, use as much braking as possible compatible with surface conditions, and when insufficient stopping distance remains, steer the aircraft away from obstructions. If it seems that a collision with obstructions is inevitable, consideration should be given to selecting the landing gear up.

If the aircraft is airborne before reaching Safety Speed, it will normally be preferable in the case of light twin engined aircraft (with their marginal performance on one engine with landing gear down and an unfeathered propeller) to immediately re-land rather than attempt what might be an impossible task, i.e. cleaning the aircraft up, feathering the correct propeller and accelerating to V_{yse} or V_{xse} from a few feet above the ground.

Alternatively, if the decision to re-land makes collision with solid obstructions inevitable, the remaining engine could be used to assist the pilot to reach a safer area for landing. But if this course of action is attempted the airspeed must not be allowed to drop below V_{mca} or loss of control will result.

ENGINE FAILURE AFTER TAKE-OFF

During training, this situation will be demonstrated and practised at a safe minimum height and at or above Safety Speed. On some engines the rapid closure of a throttle can be harmful to the engine and cause detuning of the CSU counterweights. This is because the sudden reversal of forces results in an unnatural movement of the counterweights which can weaken the metal. Therefore when closing a throttle to simulate engine failure it should not be done abruptly.

The order of actions to be taken in the event of an *'actual engine failure'* are as follows:

- Maintain directional and lateral control of the aircraft, using not more than 5° of bank towards the operating engine.
- Throttle and rpm levers should be immediately checked fully forward to ensure maximum power is being obtained.
- Landing gear (and take-off flap if used) should be retracted. However, the pilot must ensure the airspeed is adequate prior to raising flap or a 'sink' will occur. This could lead to the pilot instinctively raising the aircraft nose and losing airspeed in critical circumstances.
- If the take-off followed a 'touch and go' landing, and landing flap is still lowered, it should be raised in stages, compatible with an increase in airspeed.
- Identify the failed engine whilst achieving V_{yse}. It must be appreciated that the quicker V_{yse} is obtained, the sooner the aircraft will commence climbing. In the event that obstacles ahead make the climb out path critical, V_{xse} should be used as the climbing speed.
- The propeller of the failed engine should be feathered as soon as

possible, but because of the possibility of feathering the wrong engine, the feathering action must not be undertaken too hastily, and the following procedure should be complied with:

- Confirm correct identification of the inoperative engine by slowly closing the throttle of the engine which has been nominated as failed.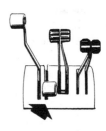
- In the event of total failure of one engine, closing the throttle of the inoperative engine will not produce any change in engine noise or any difference in the rudder pressure required in order to maintain directional control.
- In the event that partial engine failure has occurred, closing the throttle of the partially inoperative engine will result in the need for a further increase in rudder pedal pressure to maintain directional control.
- Maintain the appropriate climbing airspeed and carry out the feathering procedure. Before moving the rpm lever to the 'feather' position and the mixture to ICO, double check that the correct engine controls are being moved by referring to the closed throttle.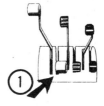

● Check for engine fire, and carry out the appropriate drills (if applicable) as laid down in the aircraft manual.
● Inform Air Traffic Control.
● Check and determine which aircraft services are still available, e.g. some aircraft have a hydraulic pump for landing gear and flap operation fitted to only one engine.
● Carefully monitor the oil temperature and pressure, and cylinder head temperature of the operating engine, and continue climbing to a safe height before manoeuvring into the circuit pattern.
● If unable to complete an immediate circuit and landing for any reason, consideration must be given to the management of the remaining fuel state and aircraft services, e.g. electrical, vacuum, etc.

CIRCUIT, APPROACH AND LANDING ON ASYMMETRIC POWER

The circuit should, where possible, conform to the standard height and traffic pattern used at the aerodrome. It will be particularly important to maintain height and if necessary, maximum power on the operating engine should be used. This will then avoid a situation where height becomes a critical factor towards the end of the downwind leg, or at the commencement of the base leg. Either of these occurrences will give the pilot additional problems and stress during the approach phase.

In relation to the maintenance of height, it should be appreciated that if necessary the speed can be reduced to the V_{yse} in an attempt to maintain height. If level flight is impossible at this airspeed, it will not be possible at any other airspeed.

The downwind RTF call and pre-landing checks should be carried out as for normal twin engined operation, but the decision to increase drag by lowering the landing gear will depend upon the performance of the aircraft at the time. When height is being maintained at less than full power, the landing gear can be lowered in the normal way during the pre-landing checks, and power increased to combat the additional drag.

In the event that full power on the operating engine is necessary to maintain height with the landing gear retracted, then clearly the lowering of the landing gear must be delayed. The actual moment at which to lower the landing gear will then be a matter for pilot judgement.

Note: It must be stressed that the position to lower the landing gear should not be considered as arbitrary, but rather it is dependent upon the actual performance of the particular aircraft at the time. If it is known that height can be maintained with the landing gear lowered, it will be preferable to lower it in the normal position during the circuit, rather than delaying its operation till later. This is because statistics reveal that most of the inadvertent 'wheels up' landings occur due to the pilot being distracted or having unusual workloads to handle during the circuit phase.

Any situation which requires a circuit, approach and landing to be conducted on asymmetric power can be considered as conducive to distraction, and if manual lowering of the gear is also necessary it will normally be inadvisable to leave this operation until the base leg, because of the time taken to lower the gear. This added workload during a period when the pilot might need all his concentration to set up a safe approach and landing could easily lead to a critical situation.

ASYMMETRIC COMMITTAL HEIGHT

Because of the significantly reduced performance when operating on one engine, consideration must be given to establishing a minimum height from which it would be safely possible to attempt a 'go round again' procedure, during an approach when the flight path will have to be changed from a descent to a climb with the aircraft in a high drag configuration.

Due to the height loss which will occur during the time that the operating engine is brought up to full power, landing gear and flap retracted, and the aircraft established in a climb at V_{yse}, a minimum height must be selected, below which the pilot should not attempt to take the aircraft round again for another circuit. This height will be compatible with the aircraft type, all up weight, altitude of the aerodrome being used, air temperature, the height of obstructions along the climb out path, and pilot competence. Nevertheless, even with a combination of the most favourable circumstances, it would be inadvisable in respect of safety considerations to make this height less than 400' agl.

BASE LEG

The base leg should usually be commenced from the normal position in the circuit. Consideration must be given to the direction of turn onto this leg in relation to the inoperative engine, i.e. if the circuit is a left hand one and the right engine has failed, the pilot will have to allow for a wider radius of turn.

When possible, the initial descent speed should not be less than V_{yse}. The reason for this is that during the descent to Asymmetric Committal Height, this gives the pilot the most favourable speed for adopting a missed approach procedure. Once below Asymmetric Committal Height a normal approach speed should be used, as from this stage onwards the pilot is committed to an approach and landing.

The use of flap whilst on the base leg will be a matter of pilot judgement in relation to distance from the runway threshold, wind component, and the aircraft height and performance capability.

When a decision is made to lower flap at any stage on the base leg or final approach, it will always be advisable to lower the required flap prior to reducing power (provided the speed is below V_{fe}). This sequence will prevent a situation occurring where, having reduced power and then lowered the flaps, it is found that the descent rate becomes greater than anticipated, and even the use of full power on the operating engine may not sufficiently reduce the increased descent rate.

FINAL APPROACH

Throughout the final approach it must be appreciated that the increased drag and reduced power available when in asymmetric flight will increase the need for anticipating an undershoot condition, and power corrections must therefore be made early rather than late.

Upon reaching the nominated Asymmetric Committal Height the approach should only be continued provided that:

- ATC have given clearance to land.
- The landing gear is locked down.
- The runway is clear.
- The aircraft is in a favourable position to continue the approach to a landing, i.e. height, airspeed and runway alignment are all satisfactory.

If all these points are established, a positive commitment to land can be made, otherwise a missed approach procedure should be initiated.

During simulated engine failure practice, both rpm levers will have been placed in the fully forward position by this stage. When it becomes clear that the aircraft can reach the touchdown point, then and only then should the final flap selection be made. However, final flap should be selected before the power on the operating engine is further reduced, as it may not be safe to do otherwise until the added drag from the landing flap has taken effect. It must also be appreciated that the decision to use full flap is a matter of pilot judgement in the prevailing circumstances.

The airspeed in the final stages of the approach should be gradually reduced to the required threshold speed for the existing conditions, but it will clearly be inadvisable to reduce speed below V_{mca} until the aircraft is at the point of 'round out' for touchdown.

If at any time after passing the Asymmetric Committal Height a baulked landing situation occurs, no problems will arise when simulated engine failure is being practised unless the simulated inoperative engine is very cold. The pilot need only apply the power available from both engines and complete a normal twin engined missed approach procedure.

However, when an actual engine failure has occurred, the pilot should not attempt a missed approach at this stage, but instead he should select a clear area of the aerodrome and complete the landing.

THE LANDING
The normal landing procedure will apply, but a yaw must be anticipated during an actual engine failure when the propeller is feathered. This will be due to the asymmetry in drag between one propeller at idling rpm and the other one feathered. For example, when the left engine is shut down and the propeller is feathered, closing the throttle of the operating engine during the 'hold off' phase will cause a slight yaw to the right.

In those aircraft which are equipped with a rudder bias spring to effect rudder trim, it may be advisable to centralise this rudder trim prior to the approach and landing, and so avoid having to apply a force on the opposite rudder pedal as the throttle of the operating engine is closed. In aircraft equipped with 'aerodynamic' rudder trim tabs this effect is markedly reduced due to the decreasing rudder trim tab force as the airspeed is decreased.

GOING ROUND AGAIN ON ASYMMETRIC POWER (MISSED APPROACH)
The speed at which the decision is made to commit the aeroplane to a landing or to overshoot should normally be V_{yse} and in any case not less than Safety Speed. The height should be such that a slow response by the pilot will still allow the aeroplane to be cleaned up (and where necessary accelerated to V_{yse}) and established in a climb with ample height still available.

Note: On no account should 'Instrument Decision Height' and its associated procedures be confused with Asymmetric Committal Height and its different purpose.

Once the decision to carry out a missed approach has been made, full throttle should be applied, the rpm lever checked fully forward, and maximum manifold pressure and rpm confirmed. Landing gear and flap should be raised whilst accelerating to or maintaining V_{yse}.

Note: Aircraft with Hydraulically Operated Landing Gear and Flap Systems:
When, due to engine failure, hydraulic power is not available to operate the landing gear or flaps, the flaps will normally retract upon selection due to external air pressure. The removal of flap drag should therefore be the first consideration, but it should also be borne in mind that the flaps may retract very quickly and a high rate of sink may be experienced.
The decision to attempt manual gear retraction will depend upon whether the aircraft has this facility and on the degree of performance available with the landing gear down. Provided climb performance is possible with the gear lowered it will normally be advisable to leave it in the lowered position and continue with a further circuit, approach and landing.

Practice Asymmetric Power Circuits
'Roller' or 'Touch and Go' landings from an approach with one engine set at zero thrust should not be attempted by pilots under training. Instructors may however require to do so, but they will need to carefully consider all the circumstances, e.g.

Is the throttled engine cold?
Has trim been applied, and if so, is directional control going to be difficult?
Is there sufficient distance available to the end of the runway and first obstruction to allow for a slower than normal acceleration?
How much flap is being used?

If a touch and go landing is to be attempted these factors (listed here so that the pilot under training has an appreciation of the problems), together with all the other prevailing circumstances, need to be assessed not later than midway along the final approach, and the student prepared for a particularly clear Hand over/Take over. The trim will probably need to be wound off immediately after touchdown and the flaps raised before power is applied.

A 'Touch and Go' when one engine has actually failed should of course never be attempted, even to avoid an accident, as the resulting circumstances will almost certainly lead to a more serious accident.

ENGINE FAILURE DURING AN ALL ENGINES APPROACH OR MISSED APPROACH

If one engine fails during a normal approach and the aircraft has descended below the nominated Asymmetric Committal Height, the approach to landing should be continued. All the factors previously covered for the single engined approach will apply, but lack of time and opportunity may preclude the feathering procedure from being carried out. Therefore greater care must be used to prevent an undershoot situation developing.

On most light twin engined aircraft the pilot will need to apply a considerable amount of power on the operating engine in order to maintain the correct airspeed and approach slope; there will also be a commensurate increase in footload. These factors will be a major point of the demonstration.

In the event that an engine fails prior to reaching the Asymmetric Committal Height, time will normally be available to identify and confirm which engine has failed and to complete the appropriate drills. Nevertheless, the decision to feather the failed engine will depend upon the pilot's workload at the time, e.g. unlike the take-off case, the pilot will be monitoring and adjusting the approach path, and obtaining ATC clearance, etc.

If the landing path is clear and other considerations point to a confirmed landing it may be preferable to leave the feathering procedure rather than to risk feathering the wrong engine. Against this must be weighed the possibility of having to commence a missed approach with an unfeathered propeller. The ultimate decisions will have to be made in accordance with the current situation.

The occurrence of an engine failure during a missed approach can produce a wide variety of circumstances. For example, an engine failure immediately following the implementation of a missed approach above Asymmetric Committal Height will give the pilot reasonable time to cope with the situation and elect to either continue with the missed approach or land.

On the other hand, an engine failure occurring at very low height and low airspeed, when the aircraft is already in a position above and along the runway with insufficient distance remaining to land safely, will create an extremely hazardous situation, particularly if the landing flap is still lowered.

More often than not a continued go around will be dangerous if the speed is below Safety Speed, and therefore it will be advisable, and probably essential, only to use the operating engine to reach the least hazardous area in which to force land.

If the speed is above Safety Speed and there are no obstructions ahead which cannot be avoided, rapid but smooth action might just enable the go around to be completed safely. Once again, Safety Speed should be regarded as a Decision Speed in assessing the action to be taken.

Note: Simulated engine failures which involve going round again from below Asymmetric Committal Height will not be practised.

Centre-Line Thrust Aircraft: Single Engined Flight

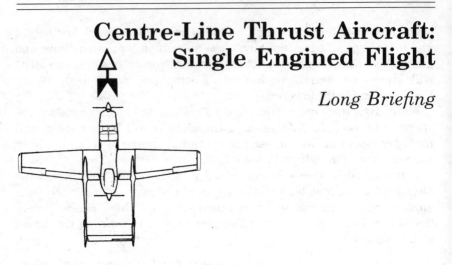

Long Briefing

CENTRE-LINE THRUST CONSIDERATIONS

Twin engined aircraft which have their engines mounted along the fuselage centre-line will not be subject to asymmetric thrust or drag. Nevertheless, although the failure of one engine will not produce problems in directional control, the significant effects of reduced performance will be present to almost the same degree as for the conventional twin engined aircraft with its engines mounted on the wings.

Another important point is that with the centre-line thrust layout, the normal control symptoms of engine failure and the determination of which engine has failed cannot be so easily recognised, e.g. asymmetric yaw will not be present.

Further to this, the arrangement of engines in a front/rear fashion, coupled with the normal layout of having the throttles, pitch levers and mixture controls in a lateral line across the quadrant in the cockpit, leads to the need for even more care when determining which pitch lever and mixture control to operate during the feathering procedure.

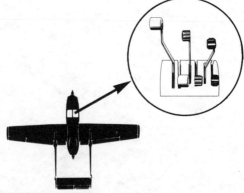

In relation to obtaining a multi engine Rating, those pilots trained in centre-line thrust aircraft will not have obtained experience of or competence at overcoming asymmetric problems, and therefore they will be issued with a Rating which carries an endorsement for use on 'Centre-Line Thrust' aircraft only.

TAXYING

It is normal to leave the front engine at idle and use the rear engine for taxying. This technique reduces the possibility of damage to the rear propeller from stones, etc., which might be thrown up when the front engine is under power.

The use of the rear engine when aligning the aircraft for take-off will also alert the pilot's attention more easily to a situation in which the rear engine has stopped.

TAKE-OFF

Take-off power should be applied to the rear engine first to check for acceleration. Careful monitoring of the manifold pressures, rpm, fuel flow, etc., should be continued throughout the take-off run and immediately afterwards to minimise the possibility of an engine failure going unrecognised at a critical stage of the flight.

SINGLE ENGINED FLIGHT

No minimum control speed will apply, but the rear engine will usually produce more power due to the position of the induction air intake, therefore the rear engine will normally be the critical engine so far as performance is concerned.

The methods of identifying an engine failure will be the reduced performance in level or climbing flight, and the changed readings of the engine gauges, e.g. tachometer, fuel flow, exhaust gas temperature, cylinder head temperature, and oil pressure and temperature.

Because no asymmetric yaw will be present it is even more important to close the throttle of the engine suspected of failing before confirming identification and proceeding with an investigation of the cause, or implementing the feathering drill.

Although no directional control problems exist if an engine fails during the take-off run or initial climb, all the problems in relation to reduced aircraft performance will be present. Therefore the need to review single engined performance figures will apply exactly as for conventional twin engined aircraft.

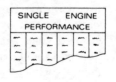

A Safety Speed will normally be quoted in the aircraft manual, but this will relate to aircraft performance rather than to any control problems. When an engine fails below the Safety Speed, the take-off should immediately be abandoned. If engine failure occurs above Safety Speed the take-off or climb out should only be continued provided the aircraft will clear all obstructions along the climb out path with the reduced available power.

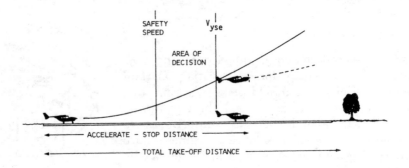

Note: Centre-Line Thrust layouts are normally only suitable for high wing aircraft, and therefore the landing gear is usually retracted into the fuselage. This may result in landing gear doors which open in such a manner that they create a marked increase in drag.

Whilst this is of no great significance during normal twin engined operations it could become of greater importance if one engine fails. For example, if one engine fails immediately after take-off and the decision is made to continue, serious consideration must be given to the acceptability of raising the landing gear, as this operation may temporarily cause a large increase of drag.

The decision to raise the landing gear in these circumstances must be balanced against the fact that the drag from the landing gear in the lowered position is normally quite small.

FLIGHT SYLLABUS

Conversion to Twin Engined Aircraft

Flight Demonstrations

Part 1   Normal Flight

Flight Demonstration

INTRODUCTION

Part 1 of the twin engined conversion flight training course covers normal flight with both engines operating. The contents of this part may be conveniently divided into three specific demonstration and practice periods as follows:

1. Aircraft Familiarisation
    Pre-Flight Preparation and Aircraft Inspection
    Starting Up Procedures
    Parking Area Procedures
    Taxying
    Pre Take-Off Procedures
    Take-Off and Initial Climb
    Introduction to the Effects of the Various Controls and Systems
    Emergency Drills (not including engine failure)
    Straight and Level Flight
    Circuit Re-Joining, Approach and Landing
2. Revision of Pre-Flight Procedures
    Taxying (including emergency drills)
    Climbing:
        Maximum Rate of Climb
        Climbing with Flap and Landing Gear Down
        Maximum Angle of Climb
    Descending:
        Powered Descent
        Descent with Flap and Landing Gear Down
        Emergency Descent
    Turning
    Stalling
    Advanced Turning
    Instrument Appreciation
3. Consolidation of:
        Take-Offs
        The Circuit

Approaches and Landings
Going Round Again

Due to the differences between multi engined aircraft, their various systems and the different methods used to operate these systems, it may be necessary to alter the order and/or content of the following demonstrations to suit the specific training aircraft, and the procedures in use at the particular flying training organisation.

The various aspects of airmanship and engine handling (as applicable to the aircraft type) should be introduced and practised at appropriate moments during the flight periods.

DEMONSTRATION 1. INTRODUCTION TO TWIN
ENGINED AIRCRAFT

Flight Lesson	Demonstration Sequence
Aircraft familiarisation and pre-flight procedures *Student participation*	Review of cockpit layout, controls and systems. External/Internal Drills and Checks, including use of the Checklist prior to and after engine starting (as applicable to the aircraft type). Importance of seating adjustment and the ability to use maximum rudder deflection when the harness is tight. Radio equipment set as required. Select auxiliary fuel tanks (if applicable).

Taxying
 Student participation
	Parking area precautions:
	   Care in use of power:
	     Greater slipstream effects
	     Hazards to smaller aircraft
	 Larger wing span and longer fuselage:
	   Clearance from other aircraft and obstructions
	 Greater inertia of aircraft:
	   Tendency towards higher taxying speed
	 Use of differential engine power.
	 Braking – Dangers of locking one wheel when turning in confined spaces.
	 Completion of all normal taxying checks, e.g. rudder travel, instrument checks, etc.
	 Additional care will be needed to straighten the nosewheel when parking

	prior to carrying out power and system checks. The need for care in positioning the aircraft: Greater power/slipstream effects and their hazard to other aircraft.

Pre take-off procedures
Power and system checks
Student participation
	Use of the checklist:
	    Larger number of checks to be carried out.
	    Selection of main fuel tanks.
	    Monitoring of engine temperatures, pressures, fuel flow, and use of cowl flaps/cooling gills, etc.
	Engine power and system checks:
	    Power settings and magneto checks.
	    The exercise of CSUs and alternate air/carburettor heat systems.
	    Alternator/Generator check.
	    Suction systems check.
	    Other checks as applicable to aircraft type.

Pre take-off checks	Use of checklist: Checks as applicable to aircraft type. Review of important speeds: ● V_{mca} ● Lift off speed and V_2 ● V_{yse} ● Field length considerations (Refusal Speed)

Take-off and initial climb
Instructor demonstration
	ATC clearance.
	Lining up on runway heading and use of power.
	Maintenance of direction.
	Note: In crosswind conditions use differential power if required.
	Monitoring of engine instruments and ASI.
	Lift off speed and V_2.
	In-Flight drills:
	    Brakes – Apply momentarily
	    Landing gear – Select up
	    Flaps – Select up (if applicable)
	    Climbing speed established
	    Power – Adjust as required
	    Re-trim
	    Above 1000′ agl – Fuel pumps 'OFF' (if applicable to aircraft type)
	    Note: Select fuel pumps OFF individually noting that fuel pressure/flow is maintained for each engine in turn.

	Power settings:
	  Manifold pressure $\big\}$ As applicable to
	  rpm type
	Re-trim.
	Adjust mixture (mixture control
	procedure will be covered later during
	this flight).
	Other systems set (as applicable to
	type).

Introduction to the effects of
the various controls and
systems
Student participation and
practice
 	
At constant power
and altitude
 	
At constant power
and altitude
	Primary controls:
	  Pressures required and rates of
	  response.
	Trimming controls:
	  Direction and response of trim control
	  movements.
	Engine controls:
	  Control of: Manifold pressure
	  rpm
	  Synchronisation of engines.
	Flap operation:
	  Limiting speed(s), V_{fe}
	  Note pitch and airspeed changes
	  relative to various flap settings.
	Landing gear operation:
	  Limiting speed(s), V_{lo} and V_{le}.
	  Selection method.
	  Indicating System(s).
	  Note pitch and airspeed changes
	  when the landing gear is operated.
	Fuel System – Fuel selection during
	flight:
	  Sequence of tank selection:
	    Main tanks
	    Auxiliary tanks
	    Use of electric fuel pumps
	    Operation of the fuel crossfeed
	    system
	Mixture control:
	  Use of fuel flow and/or exhaust gas
	  temperature gauges.
	Other systems:
	  Use of alternate air or carburettor
	  heat.
	    Carburettor air temperature gauge
	    indications.
	    Effect on manifold pressure.
	  Operation of cowl flaps/cooling gills.
	  Operation of cabin heating,
	  ventilation, and windscreen defrost
	  systems.
	  Operation of other controls and
	  systems as applicable to aircraft type,

	e.g. airframe and propeller de-icing/anti-icing, auto pilot, pressurisation, oxygen, etc.
Emergency drills (excluding engine failure) *Student participation and practice*	Malfunction of systems: Rectification procedures and drills (as applicable to aircraft type) Flaps Landing gear Alternators/Generators Vacuum system Static system – Alternate source Other systems as applicable to the aircraft type
Straight and level flight from a specific cruising airspeed *Student practice*	Select and practise straight and level flight at two different cruising speeds (the second airspeed should be below the V_{fe}). Readjust power to obtain each airspeed in turn and re-trim. Changing the aircraft configuration whilst maintaining a constant altitude: Ensure the airspeed is within the flap limiting range. Select 10° to 20° of flap. Readjust power to maintain airspeed and note the changed attitude in pitch. Reduce airspeed to below V_{lo}/V_{le}. Select landing gear 'down' and readjust power to maintain airspeed. Note new attitude in pitch. Retract flaps and landing gear. Return the aircraft to normal cruising flight.
Performance considerations	Power selection for obtaining best range/endurance as applicable from the figures given in the aircraft manual.
Circuit rejoining, approach and landing *Student participation*	Note method of positioning the aircraft into the circuit. Review of drills, checks and procedures. Demonstration circuit, approach and landing.
Running down and switching off	Use of the aircraft checklist.

At this stage the student will have participated in the demonstrations and had practice at operating those controls which affect the aircraft attitude and performance.

COMPLETION STANDARDS

Upon the completion of this flight lesson, the student should have obtained a good understanding of the required pre-flight preparation, start up and taxying procedures, including an introduction to the aircraft manual and use of the checklist.

Before proceeding to the next air exercise the student will need to be proficient at operating the various systems applicable to the aircraft being used, whilst maintaining control of the aircraft's attitude, airspeed and altitude. He will also need to demonstrate competence in handling the emergency procedures (excluding those which relate to engine failure).

DEMONSTRATION 2.   CONVERSION TO TWIN ENGINED AIRCRAFT

Flight Lesson	Demonstration Sequence

Consolidation period of pre-flight procedures
Student practice
	External/Internal drills and checks:
	  Engine starting
	  Taxying
	Steering and/or brake failure procedures.
	Engine power and system checks.

Take-off and initial climb Student practice	Pre take-off checks. Review of important speeds. ATC clearance. Lining up and application of power. Maintenance of aircraft direction. Engine power and system checks during the take-off run. Lift off speed and V_2 Adoption of best rate of climb speed. Landing gear/flap retraction procedure. Reduction of manifold pressure and rpm to climbing power. Re-trim. Above 1000′ – fuel pumps off (as applicable to aircraft type). Cruise climb airspeed as required. Final trim adjustments.
Climbing From level flight at cruising power Student participation and practice	Fuel system requirements, re-select tanks as necessary. Mixture as required. Power selection as applicable to aircraft type:

	rpm $\left.\begin{array}{l}\\ \end{array}\right\}$ Increase to Manifold pressure $\quad$ Climb setting Adopt climbing attitude. Note airspeed and re-adjust attitude as necessary. Re-trim: Elevator trim $\qquad$ Rudder trim $\qquad$ Aileron trim (as applicable) Re-synchronise engines. Adjust throttles to maintain manifold pressure with increase of altitude (as applicable to aircraft type). Mixture – adjust as recommended in the aircraft manual. Monitor: $\quad$ Oil temperature $\quad$ Oil pressure $\quad$ Fuel flow/pressure $\quad$ Cylinder head temperature $\qquad$ Adjust cowl flaps/cooling gills (as necessary) $\quad$ Cabin pressurisation (as applicable) $\quad$ High Altitude: $\qquad$ Use of electric fuel pumps and oxygen systems above 10 000'.
Levelling off	Adopt attitude in pitch Power selection: $\quad$ Manifold pressure $\left.\begin{array}{l}\\ \\ \end{array}\right\}$ Cruise setting $\quad$ rpm Re-synchronise engines Re-trim. Attitude and power adjustments as necessary to achieve selected cruising airspeed. Re-adjust mixture controls. Final trim adjustments.
Climbing with flap and landing gear down *Student participation and practice*	From level flight with take-off flap and landing gear down – adopt climbing power and best rate of climb airspeed. Select flap and landing gear up, noting trim changes. Re-adjust pitch attitude to maintain best rate of climb airspeed. Reduce manifold pressure and rpm to cruise climb power. Re-adjust pitch attitude for the cruise climb airspeed. Re-trim and synchronise engines. Return the aircraft to normal cruising flight.
Maximum angle of climb	Select maximum climbing power and readjust pitch attitude for the maximum angle of climb airspeed.

	Re-trim. Return the aircraft to normal cruising flight.

Descending
Student participation and
practice
 	
Select a specific airspeed and
rate of descent
	Complete the pre-descent checks:
	    Fuel – selection
	    Mixture – adjustment
	    Cowl flaps/cooling gills – adjustment
	    Altimeter setting – as required
	Power selection:
	    Manifold pressure ⎤ Select as
	    rpm ⎦ appropriate
	Adjust aircraft attitude to achieve the selected airspeed and re-trim.
	When the correct airspeed has been achieved note the rate of descent.
	Re-adjust power and attitude as required and re-trim.
	During the descent it will be necessary to carefully monitor the cylinder head temperatures.
	Mixture will need to be adjusted as required.
	Return the aircraft to straight and level flight and re-trim.
	Re-adjust mixture and cowl flaps/cooling gills as necessary.

Descending with flap and *landing gear lowered* *Student practice*	Adopt a normal powered descent at 500 fpm, with the airspeed within the flap and landing gear lowered range. Select 10° to 15° of flap and note attitude and trim change. Maintain original airspeed and note the increased rate of descent. Select landing gear down and note attitude and trim change. Maintain original airspeed and note the increased rate of descent. Return the aircraft to straight and level flight. Raise flaps in stages and retract landing gear. Adopt normal cruising flight.
Emergency descent *Student participation and* *practice*	Adopt the procedure recommended in the aircraft manual.
Turning *Student practice*	Practise normal level turns onto selected headings. Practise climbing turns onto selected headings. Practise descending turns onto selected headings.

Slow flight and stalling *Student participation and* *practice*	Practice of controlled flight at low airspeeds: Adopt level flight at a low airspeed (not below V_{sse} or equivalent for aircraft type). Practise slow flight in the straight and level condition. Practise slow flight at a controlled rate of climb. Practise slow flight at a controlled rate of descent. Practice of slow flight during turning manoeuvres in level, climbing and descending flight. Repeat the above manoeuvres with flaps and landing gear lowered.
Stalling from level flight, *clean configuration and no* *power* *Instructor demonstration* *Refer to the particular* *aircraft manual for* *information on any stalling* *limitations or restrictions*	Complete the safety checks, including the selection of an appropriate rpm. Symptoms of the stall. The stall – note the handling characteristics of the aircraft type. The use of the flying controls and power during the recovery to level flight. Note the height loss. Student Practice.
Stalling from level flight, *clean configuration and a* *low cruise power selected*	Complete the safety checks including the selection of an appropriate rpm. Symptoms of the stall. The stall – note the handling characteristics of the aircraft type. The use of the flying controls and power during the recovery to level flight. Note the height loss. Student Practice.
Stalling from both straight *and turning flight with flap* *and landing gear lowered*	Repeat previous stalling exercises and note any significant changes in stalling characteristics. Student Practice.
Recovery from the stall at the *incipient stage – from both* *straight and turning flight* *in the clean configuration* *Recovery from the stall at the* *incipient stage – from both* *straight and turning flight* *with the aircraft in the* *approach configuration* *Recovery from the stall* *during change of aircraft* *configuration*	Repeat the previous stalling exercises but initiate recovery action just prior to the stall occurring. Student practice Repeat the previous exercise with the aircraft in the 'approach configuration'. Student practice. Enter the stall with landing gear and flap lowered. At the point of recovery select flaps up and note any change in stall recovery

	characteristics. Student practice
Advanced turning *Student practice during level flight*	Adjust rpm as applicable. *LOOKOUT* Practice of steep turns with emphasis on control co-ordination, a safe airspeed and constant altitude.
Student practice during descending flight	Place the aircraft in a descent and practise steep descending turns with emphasis upon control of bank and airspeed.
Student practice during climbing flight	Place the aircraft in a climb and practise steep climbing turns with emphasis upon control of bank and airspeed.
Recovery from unusual attitudes	From straight and level flight adopt a steeply banked attitude with the nose high.
Student participation and practice	Recovery: Simultaneous pitch and bank adjustment to straight flight at a safe airspeed. From straight and level flight adopt a steeply banked attitude with the nose low. Recovery: Prompt power reduction and removal of bank. Return the aircraft to the straight and level attitude.
Stalling in the turn *Student participation and practice* *Refer to the particular aircraft manual for information regarding any stalling limitations or restrictions*	From straight and level flight at a speed below V_a for the aircraft type. Enter and maintain a level turn at a low airspeed. Firmly increase the back pressure on the control column. Limit bank angle to approximately 40°. Recover as soon as the stall symptoms occur. *Note*: During this demonstration care must be used to avoid exceeding the limiting load factor.
Instrument appreciation *Student practice*	A general review of instrument flight should be made at this stage. The student should practise straight and level flight, followed by climbing, descending and turning manoeuvres. These should initially be conducted as a precision exercise, followed by practice under the 'hood'.

The circuit, approach and landing Student participation or practice	Review and practice of the circuit, approach and normal landing.

COMPLETION STANDARDS

Upon the completion of this flight lesson, the student must have demonstrated his ability to cope with the various emergency drills as applicable to the aircraft type (but excluding single engined flight), and be able to control the aircraft with reasonable accuracy in Straight and Level, Climbing, Descending and Turning Flight.

The student must also be capable of controlling the aircraft during Slow Flight within 10 knots of the nominated speed and 200' of the required altitude.

During Advanced Turns, the angle of bank and airspeed must be relatively constant, and any variation of altitude should not exceed 200'.

Stalling and Unusual Attitude Recoveries must be positively executed without excessive loss of altitude.

DEMONSTRATION 3. CONVERSION TO TWIN ENGINED AIRCRAFT

Flight Lesson	Demonstration Sequence
The take-off, circuit, approach and landing The take-off and initial climb	Pre take-off checks completed. Review important speeds: V_{mca} Lift off speed and V_2 V_{yse} Refusal Speed Approach path and runway clear. ATC liaison. Line up on the runway centre line with the nosewheel straight and confirm correct runway heading. Apply initial power against the brakes. At approximately 50% power note: Correct fuel flow/pressure on both engines. Release the brakes. Smoothly increase the power to the maximum permitted.

	Maintain direction with rudder.
	Ensure that the manifold pressure and rpm limitations are not exceeded.
	Confirm:
	Airspeed increasing.
	Engine oil pressure, temperature, and cylinder head temperature are within correct limits.
	Fuel flow/pressure – correct readings.
Lift off	Lift off at V_2 or earlier (dependent upon the particular aircraft type).
	Accelerate through V_2 to V_y and continue the climb to circuit height.
	Brakes – apply temporarily.
	Landing Gear – select UP.
	Flaps (if used) – select UP.
	Adjust power:
	Manifold pressure ⎫ Climbing power rpm ⎭
	Re-trim and synchronise engines.
Whichever technique is applicable	⎧ Continue the climb onto the crosswind leg and level off at circuit height, or ⎨ Continue the climb to circuit height, level off and turn onto the crosswind leg. ⎩
	Note: Throughout the whole circuit procedure, from take-off to touchdown, care must be used to space the aircraft at a safe distance from slower aircraft. Normally a wider circuit pattern is used to allow more time for the appropriate drills and to place the aircraft outside the path used by smaller aircraft.
Downwind leg	Upon completion of the crosswind leg, *LOOKOUT*, and turn downwind.
	Frequently monitor the height and make the RTF call.
	Ensure the airspeed is below the V_{lo}/V_{fe}.
	Complete the pre-landing checks.
	Adjust power as necessary to overcome the drag from the lowered landing gear (and flaps if used).
	Confirm the landing gear is locked in the 'down' position.
	Note the position to turn onto the base leg.
Powered approaches and landings	*LOOKOUT*, followed by a medium turn onto the base leg.

The base leg

Allow for the drift (if applicable).
Nominate an 'Asymmetric Committal Height' and select the required power for the descent.
Select the flaps as required and establish the specific descent airspeed. Re-trim.
Adjust power and/or increase the flap setting as necessary to control the rate of descent.
Note: Remember that lookout invariably suffers when added workloads occur, for example, during the conversion period onto a different aircraft type, or in any unusual situation. In these circumstances it will be essential to think more positively about lookout, rather than to rely upon an established habit.

The final approach

Maintain a careful *LOOKOUT* and establish the final approach path.
Select a touchdown zone, and continue to adjust power and flap as required, to control the desired rate of descent.
RTF call 'Finals – 3 Greens'.
Note: If an engine fails below the nominated Asymmetric Committal Height, the approach should be continued and a landing completed.

The landing

Adjust power and attitude to arrive at the pre-selected touchdown area.
Power should be reduced gradually during the flare and the throttles closed just prior to touchdown.
Note: Premature closure of the throttles may cause a rapid sink and result in a hard landing.
Under normal conditions the initial touchdown should be accomplished on the main wheels, after which the nosewheel should be gently lowered onto the runway.

After landing

Maintain directional control by use of the rudder and differential braking.
Note: Some engines may be prone to stopping after landing due to an over rich mixture when the throttles are closed and the electric fuel pumps are ON. In these circumstances the fuel

	pumps should be switched to the 'Low' position or 'Off', during the landing roll.
	'After Landing Checks', including the raising of flaps, should be completed when the aircraft is clear of the runway/landing area and stationary.
Mislanding	In the event of a mislanding:
	Apply full power and when the situation is safely under control, establish the aircraft in a climb. Retract the landing gear, and raise the flaps in stages compatible with obtaining a safe *airspeed* and height.
Going round again	If a roller landing is being carried out, care will be needed (on certain aircraft) to prevent the occurrence of 'wheelbarrowing'. When using an aircraft which is prone to this it may be advisable to raise the flaps to the take-off position, after the landing has been made and prior to increasing the power for the take-off.
	Bear in mind that with flap down the aircraft will tend to become airborne at a lower airspeed. If the aircraft is allowed to leave the ground below V_{mca} extreme care will be needed. In these circumstances the airspeed must be allowed to increase before any gain in height is attempted.

COMPLETION STANDARDS

Upon completion of this flight lesson the student must be capable of safely carrying out the circuit procedures and the various types of normal take-offs, approaches and landings. The student must also be capable of implementing the procedure required in the event of a missed approach or mislanding situation.

Part 2 Asymmetric Flight

Flight Demonstration

INTRODUCTION

Part 2 of the twin engined conversion flight training course covers the abnormal situation of one engine failing during any stage of flight. The contents of this part may be conveniently divided into three specific demonstration and practice periods as follows:

1. Flight on Asymmetric Power
    Effects and Recognition of Engine Failure During Level Flight
    Maintenance of Control and Identification of the Failed Engine
    Effects and Recognition of Engine Failure During Turns:
    Methods of Control and Identification
    Effects of Varying Airspeed and Power During Asymmetric
    Flight
2. Minimum Control Speeds (V_{mc})
    Effect of Bank Angle upon V_{mc}
    Effect of Feathering upon V_{mc}
    Effect of the Take-Off Configuration upon V_{mc}
    Engine Failure Procedures
    Feathering and Unfeathering Procedures
    Control and Performance During the Take-Off and Approach
    Phases
    Significance of Safety Speed (V_2)
    Significance of Asymmetric Committal Height
3. Engine Failure During Take-Off
    Engine Failure After Take-Off
    Circuit, Approach and Landing on Asymmetric Power
    Engine Failure During a Normal (all engines) Approach or
    Missed Approach

Due to the differences between multi engined aircraft, their various systems and the different methods used to operate these systems, it may be necessary to alter the order and/or content of the following demonstrations to suit the specific training aircraft, and the procedures in use at the particular flying training organisation.

The various aspects of airmanship and engine handling (as applicable to the aircraft type) should be introduced and practised at appropriate moments during the flight periods.

DEMONSTRATION 1.   ASYMMETRIC FLIGHT

Flight Lesson	Demonstration Sequence

Flight on one engine
Safety note:
    This demonstration
    must not be carried out
    below 3000' agl
Instructor demonstration
and student participation
	Feather the left propeller and adopt single engined straight and level flight. Note the power required for level flight at a selected single engine airspeed. The trimming controls are used to relieve control pressures as in normal flight.
	Balanced flight can be achieved.
	All normal turning manoeuvres can be safely conducted.
	Adopt climbing flight at the maximum power permitted on the operating engine.
	Note the low rate of climb.
	Return to level flight.

Optional procedures if the aircraft manual does not quote a 'zero thrust' setting	Prior to unfeathering the inoperative engine, set a high cruise rpm on the operating engine and note the manifold pressure required to achieve a selected airspeed in level flight. Maintain level flight and constant power on the operating engine and restart the left engine. Increase the manifold pressure on the left engine and when the aircraft has been retrimmed, note the manifold pressure required on the left engine to achieve the previously selected single engine airspeed in level flight. This manifold pressure is the approximate 'Zero Thrust' setting. Return to normal cruising flight.

Effects and recognition of engine failure during level flight
Instructor demonstration
	With the aircraft correctly trimmed in level flight, maintain a good lookout and remove hands and feet from the flying controls.
	Gradually close one throttle and note:
	    A yaw, roll and spiral descent
	    towards the idling engine will occur.
	Return to normal twin engined flight.
	Close the other throttle and note that

	the same characteristics occur but in the opposite direction. Repeat the previous actions, closing each throttle alternately, and note the flight instrument indications associated with failure of one engine.
Maintenance of control during engine failure *From straight and level flight* *Instructor demonstration and student participation*	Gently throttle back the left engine whilst using rudder to prevent yaw and ailerons to maintain lateral level. Use elevators and power to maintain altitude. Note that balanced flight and a constant heading can be maintained. Return the aircraft to normal flight. Gently throttle back the right engine and repeat the above demonstration. Return the aircraft to normal flight. At this stage the student should practise maintaining balance, heading and altitude whilst the instructor closes each throttle alternately. Note the *'Idle Leg – Idle Engine'* method of identifying which engine has failed. Return the aircraft to normal flight.
Identification of which engine has failed *Student practice*	The student will now practise the maintenance of balance, heading and altitude whilst at the same time identifying which engine has been throttled back. During this practice the 'engine instrument indications' of engine failure (as against those seen by throttling back) will be itemised by the instructor.
Partial failure of one engine	Flight and engine instrument indications are of particular importance during IMC or when only a partial power loss of one engine occurs. In the event of an actual engine failure, the final confirmation of which engine has failed must be established by closing the throttle of the engine nominated as failed.
Supplementary recovery procedure *Student participation and practice*	From level cruising flight at a low airspeed, close one throttle. Allow the aircraft to yaw and then close the other throttle. Note that control is easily regained but that altitude is lost. *Summary*: If an engine fails during flight at a very low airspeed

	(when the rudder may be insufficiently effective in controlling yaw), closing the throttle of the operating engine and lowering the aircraft nose to gain airspeed will enable the pilot to regain directional control.
Effects and recognition of engine failure during turns Instructor demonstration and student participation	Enter a moderately banked left turn at normal cruising airspeed. Close the right throttle and note: When the outside engine fails the aircraft will yaw and roll out of the turn and enter a turn and spiral descent in the opposite direction. Return to normal straight and level flight. Re-enter a left turn, close the left throttle and note: When the inside engine fails the aircraft will yaw and roll rapidly into the turn direction, the bank angle will steepen and a spiral descent will occur. *Summary*: In both cases the visual indications will be yaw, followed by a roll and a spiral descent. The flight instrument indications may be more difficult to interpret than when in straight and level flight. Return the aircraft to normal cruising flight.
The instructor will mask the throttle quadrant and close the throttles alternately Student practice	From moderately banked turns in both directions. During each simulated engine failure the student must correctly identify which engine has failed whilst maintaining control of the aircraft. The student should initially maintain the turn and increase power as necessary to maintain altitude. Following this the aircraft should be returned to straight and level flight on one engine. *Summary*: At normal cruising or higher airspeeds, control of the aircraft following an engine failure in a turn will not present a problem. However,

	at lower airspeeds it may be necessary to reduce power on the operating engine to more quickly re-establish control of the aircraft.
Effects of varying airspeed and power *Varying the airspeed at a constant power setting* *Student participation and practice*	From straight and level flight at cruising power and airspeed. Close the left throttle whilst preventing yaw, use sufficient aileron to maintain lateral level and confirm a constant heading is being maintained. Maintain altitude and note the airspeed in asymmetric level flight for the power setting being used. Note the rudder deflection and control force. Raise the aircraft nose and gradually reduce the airspeed to V_{yse}. As the airspeed is decreased, a larger amount of rudder deflection will be needed to prevent yaw. Also note that a greater aileron deflection will be required to keep the wings level. Return to twin engined flight at V_{yse}. *Summary:* An engine failure at low airspeed will lead to the need for a large rudder deflection if yaw is to be prevented.
Varying the power at a constant airspeed *Student participation and practice*	Maintain V_{yse} and close one throttle. Hold the wings level and maintain balance. Select climbing power on the operative engine. Note that more rudder deflection will be required to maintain balance. Note that more aileron deflection will be required to keep the wings level. Return to normal cruising flight. *Summary:* A reduction of airspeed or an increase of power will result in an increase of control deflection to maintain balance with the wings level. The largest amount of control deflection and force will be required at a low airspeed and high power.
High airspeed and low power *Student practice*	From straight and level flight place the aircraft in a trimmed descent at cruising speed and with a low power setting.

	Remove hands and feet from the flying controls.
	Partially reduce the power of one engine and note:
	    Symptoms of asymmetry are less marked, leading to the possibility of partial power failure going unnoticed during a descent.
	Continue to reduce power to idling on the selected engine and note:
	    Even when one engine fails completely the visual, feel and instrument 'asymmetric symptoms' are not very apparent when the airspeed is high and power is low.
	Return to normal cruising flight.

COMPLETION STANDARDS

Upon completion of this flight lesson the student should be able to recognise the occurrence of engine failure, and identify the inoperative engine, during level, turning and descending flight.

The student must also have obtained a clear appreciation of the effect of airspeed and the power being used on the operating engine, in their relation to the directional control and balance of the aircraft.

DEMONSTRATION 2.   ASYMMETRIC FLIGHT

Flight Lesson	*Demonstration Sequence*
Minimum control speeds *Instructor demonstration* *and student participation* *A propeller will not be* *feathered during this* *demonstration*	Place the aircraft in straight and level trimmed flight at an altitude normally not above 2000' for aircraft with non supercharged/turbocharged engines. Raise the aircraft nose and reduce airspeed to V_{yse}. Select maximum permitted rpm and manifold pressure on the right engine. Gradually close the left throttle whilst maintaining balance, heading and wings level. Slowly raise the aircraft nose and reduce the airspeed. Note the airspeed at which maximum rudder deflection is being applied and when directional control can no longer be maintained.

Note: The effects of complete loss of control will not be demonstrated. This aspect has already been covered in the Long Briefing

Lower the aircraft nose to increase airspeed and decrease the power on the operating engine until positive directional control is fully regained. The lowest airspeed achieved before directional control was lost is the V_{mc} for this flight condition.

Note: If the aircraft stalls before the minimum control speed is reached, try the demonstration with the flap and landing gear down.

Repeat the above demonstration closing the right throttle and note the minimum control speed with the left engine operating.

Summary: Comparing the minimum control speeds achieved in these two demonstrations will establish the critical engine for the aircraft type, i.e. the engine which, when failed, gives the highest V_{mc}.

Return to normal cruising flight. Student practice at finding the minimum control speed.

Effect of bank angle upon V_{mc}
Student participation and practice

Repeat the previous demonstration with the critical engine throttled back. Before the airspeed reaches the previous V_{mc} use 5° of bank towards the operating engine. Note the slightly lower V_{mc}.

Return the aircraft to normal cruising flight. Student practice.

Effect of feathering in relation to V_{mc}

The student should now practise the previous demonstration but with zero thrust manifold pressure set on the idling engine.

Note: A lower minimum control speed will be achieved if the failed engine is feathered.

Effect of the take-off configuration upon the V_{mc}
Student participation and practice

Reduce the airspeed below V_{lo}/V_{fe} and lower landing gear and take-off flap. Set zero thrust on the left engine and select maximum permitted rpm and manifold pressure on the operating engine.

Gradually reduce the airspeed by raising the aircraft nose and establish the minimum control speed in the take-off configuration.

	Note whether any adverse control characteristics occur. Student practice.

Engine failure procedures
Student participation and
practice
	From cruising flight the instructor should close one throttle (or alternatively move the mixture control of one engine to the ICO position).
	Immediate actions:
	  Control yaw whilst maintaining a safe speed and altitude.
	  Select additional power (as required) on the operating engine.
	  When control is established:
	    Identify the inoperative engine.
	    Confirm identification by slowly closing the throttle of the engine which has been nominated as failed.
	When confirmation is established, identify the cause of failure:
	  Fuel tank correctly selected.
	  Check fuel quantity remaining in the selected tank.
	    Re-select fuel tanks – as applicable.
	  Fuel flow/pressure check.
	  Fuel pump – Switch ON (or confirm ON, as applicable).
	    Select alternate air/carburettor heat.
	    Mixture – adjust if necessary.
	    Oil pressure and oil temperature check.
	    Cylinder head temperature check.
	    Magnetos – both ON.
	    Any other checks as applicable to the aircraft type.

If the cause of failure cannot
be rectified
	Implement the feathering drill (as laid down for the aircraft type).
	Use of checklist to confirm the inoperative engine has been correctly secured:
	  Fuel selector OFF
	  Fuel pump OFF
	  Magneto switches OFF
	  Alternator/generator OFF
	  Cowl flap on the failed engine closed to the minimum drag position
	  Reduce all drag to a minimum and maintain altitude if practicable
	  Complete any additional items as applicable to the particular aircraft type, e.g. propeller synchrophaser

	OFF, etc.
	Final trim adjustments as required.
	Subsequent actions in relation to the operating engine and other services:
	rpm and manifold pressure set as required.
	Adjust mixture as required.
	Auxiliary fuel pump ON (as applicable).
	Review cylinder head temperature and adjust cowl gills/shutters as required.
	Monitor oil temperature and pressure at frequent intervals.
	Monitor alternator/generator charge rate and reduce electrical load as necessary.
	Monitor suction supply to the flight instruments.
	Fuel tank selection as required.
	Note: If no apparent cause of engine failure can be found, caution should be used if contemplating the crossfeeding of fuel to balance the fuel tank contents. The failure may have been caused by contaminated fuel.
Re-planning the stage length of the flight	Consider the best course of action for single engined flight, i.e. whether to continue to planned destination or proceed to an alternative aerodrome. The decision should be based upon the following factors:
	Weather conditions
	Distance to go
	Terrain to be overflown
	Aircraft single engined performance
	Remaining services supplied by the operating engine
	Fuel state (the amount of usable fuel)
	Availability of ATC services and alternate aerodromes
	In relation to single engined performance the following factors should be reviewed:
	Single engine ceiling
	Aircraft manoeuvrability
	The operating engine – limitations
	Methods of handling the fuel system and other services
Unfeathering procedure	Review procedure for unfeathering – checklist.
	Implement unfeathering drill (as

Following an actual engine failure – consideration must be given to the advisability of unfeathering	applicable for aircraft type). Engine handling considerations: Monitor engine gauges immediately after re-starting, and allow the unfeathered engine to warm up before normal power is resumed. Complete the after starting drills, e.g. alternator/generator ON, etc., as applicable to aircraft type. Adjust the cowl flaps/cooling gills and mixture as required. Re-trim for normal flight. Student practice of feathering and unfeathering procedures. Use of 'Touch Drills' when applicable. At this stage the student should be placed in simulated conditions of single engined flight, and make decisions regarding the best course of action with regard to re-planning the remainder of the flight.
Control and performance during an engine failure in the take-off phase *Student practice*	Adopt normal cruising flight at approximately 2000′ agl and away from the circuit. Lower the landing gear and take-off flap. Reduce airspeed to the Safety Speed or V_{sse} (whichever is the higher). Increase power (rpm and manifold pressure) on both engines to the maximum permitted. Close one throttle, or mixture control to ICO to simulate engine failure. *Note*: At the Safety Speed (or above) directional and lateral control can be safely maintained. Raise the landing gear and flap. Select 'zero thrust' on the idling engine. Adopt V_{yse} and re-trim. *Note*: The climb performance and the significance of achieving at least the Safety Speed at lift off or before entering a positive climb.
Asymmetric committal height *Student practice*	Set the aircraft into a descent with landing gear and flap lowered. Set 'zero thrust' on one engine. Adopt a typical approach airspeed (below V_{yse}) for the aircraft type. At a nominated altitude adopt the missed approach procedure:

	Apply full power on the operating engine. Raise landing gear and flaps. Adopt V_{yse}. Note the altitude loss between initiating the missed approach procedure and establishing a positive rate of climb. Repeat the above demonstration commencing at V_{yse}, and note the smaller height loss involved between applying power and climbing away. *Note*: The importance of selecting a safe height below which a missed approach should not be initiated, and the value of maintaining at least V_{yse} until this height is reached during an asymmetric approach.

COMPLETION STANDARDS

Upon completion of this flight lesson the student must have demonstrated his ability to clearly recognise the symptoms of approaching V_{mc}, and additionally be able to control the aircraft at this airspeed.

The student will also have to show that he understands how various factors can change V_{mc}, and display competence at feathering and unfeathering procedures, and controlling the aircraft during simulated engine failure in the take-off configuration using maximum permitted engine power.

Finally, he will need to demonstrate his understanding of the principle and purpose of establishing an Asymmetric Committal Height.

DEMONSTRATION 3.   ASYMMETRIC FLIGHT

Flight Lesson	*Demonstration Sequence*
Procedure following engine failure during the take-off phase *Student participation*	Pre take-off checks completed. Review important speeds: V_{mca} Lift-off speed and V_2 V_{yse}

Engine failure during takeoff

Refusal speed
Approach path and runway clear.
ATC clearance.
Normal take-off commenced.
Note: This demonstration may only be
    shown provided ample distance is
    available and the take-off surface
    is suitable for firm braking action
    to be applied.
ATC liaison.
Shortly after full power has been
applied, close one throttle to simulate
engine failure.
Immediate actions:
    Close the throttle of the operating
    engine.
    Maintain direction by use of rudder
    and differential braking action.
    Apply firm braking action compatible
    with available distance remaining.

*Engine failure after lift off
(Training procedure)*

At a safe height, and at or above Safety
Speed or V_{sse} (whichever is higher),
close one throttle to simulate engine
failure.
Immediate actions:
    Maintain directional control with
    rudder.
    Use not more than 5° of bank towards
    the operating engine.
    Throttle (operating engine) and rpm
    levers fully forward.
    Maintain a safe airspeed and select
    landing gear and flaps (if used) up.
    Identify failed engine whilst adopting
    V_{yse}.
Confirm which engine has failed by
slowly closing the throttle of the
identified engine.
Simulate the feathering procedure by
using 'Touch Drills' and selecting 'zero
thrust' on the idling engine.
Continue the climb on one engine to the
desired circuit height.
Note rate of climb.
Student practice
Note: At least one single engined climb
    to the downwind position must be
    made.
    Thereafter, and in the interests of
    engine handling, the single
    engined climb may be
    discontinued after the student has

	clearly established full control and a positive rate of climb. A different engine should be throttled back for each practice.
Circuit, approach and landing on asymmetric power	At an early stage on the downwind leg, close one throttle and simulate engine failure. Maintain control and identify the failed engine. Maintain constant height and a safe airspeed, increasing the power on the operating engine as necessary. Confirm identification of the failed engine. Review services remaining, e.g. hydraulic system, etc. Maintain a careful lookout and identify cause of failure. Rectify if possible. For the purpose of this practice assume rectification is not possible: Simulate feathering procedure using 'Touch Drills' and select 'zero thrust' on the idling engine. Continue the circuit on one engine: Trim as required. Maintain height – power as required. RTF call – PAN message. Complete pre-landing checks. *Note 1*: If excess power is available to overcome landing gear drag and maintain height, it will normally be advisable to select landing gear down during the pre-landing checks. If marginal or insufficient power is available to maintain height, leave the selection of landing gear down until later. *Note 2*: If manual lowering of the landing gear is required this should wherever possible be commenced prior to turning onto the base leg. *Note 3*: Pay particular attention to the maintenance of a constant height until the base leg is commenced. Provided height can be maintained, a normal size circuit should be carried out with the base leg turn completed in the normal position.

The base leg

Maintain a careful lookout and note the position of any other aircraft in the circuit.

Review which engine has failed in relation to the direction of turn onto the base leg, e.g.

If a left hand circuit is being carried out and the right engine has failed, an allowance must be made for the reduced rate and wider radius of turn onto the base leg and final approach.

Nominate an 'Asymmetric Committal Height' (normally not below 400′ agl).

Maintain an airspeed at or above V_{yse}.

Assess descent path distance to the runway threshold in relation to the wind strength, and if the situation permits, select the first stage of flap. If the power available is marginal leave the initial flap selection until later.

Adjust power and/or flap as necessary to commence the descent.

Adjust the rate of descent to ensure a minimum height of 600′ agl for the turn onto the final approach.

The final approach

RTF call 'Finals – 3 Greens'.

Maintain an approach speed (not below V_{yse}) until reaching Asymmetric Committal Height.

As Asymmetric Committal Height is approached check the following:

- Landing clearance is obtained from ATC.
- The runway is clear.
- The landing gear is locked down.
- The height, speed and runway alignment are favourable for the approach to be continued.

At Asymmetric Committal Height 'Decision'.

Adjust the approach path as necessary and select flap compatible with the situation.

Note: Landing flap must not be used until it is clearly established that the aircraft will safely reach the runway threshold.

When below the Asymmetric Committal Height the airspeed should be gradually adjusted to arrive over the runway threshold at the selected airspeed.

Note: In turbulent weather conditions, use an increased threshold speed

The landing	if runway length permits. Final flap selection (as applicable). The normal landing procedure will apply, but a yaw towards the operating engine must be anticipated when the throttle is closed during a landing with the failed engine feathered. This is due to the drag from the operating engine when in the idling condition. *Note*: When practising with zero thrust set, it will be necessary to close both throttles together just prior to touchdown.
Going round again on asymmetric power	From the approach to land (at or above Asymmetric Committal Height). Full power selected on the operating engine. Confirm maximum rpm and manifold pressure being achieved. Maintain heading and lateral level. Establish V_{yse}. Select landing gear up. $\quad\left.\begin{array}{l}\text{In the order}\\\text{required for}\\\text{the}\end{array}\right.$ Select flap (if used) up. $\quad\left.\begin{array}{l}\text{particular}\\\text{situation and}\\\text{aircraft type.}\end{array}\right.$ Establish a positive rate of climb. *Note*: If the landing gear/flap system is inoperative, it will normally be advisable to select flaps up first as the aerodynamic pressure will retract them. Consideration can then be given to the advisability of manually raising the landing gear. Climb straight ahead or to one side of the runway (as applicable). At a safe height commence re-positioning the aircraft onto the downwind leg.
Engine failure during a normal (all engines operating) approach	Maintain directional control and a safe approach airspeed. Decision to continue with the approach and landing. Continue the approach if below the nominated Asymmetric Committal Height.
Engine failure during a normal (all engines operating) missed approach *Note: Sudden engine failure*	Maintain directional control, wings level (or not more than 5° of bank) towards the operating engine. Ensure that maximum power, rpm and

at this stage will produce a rapid and powerful yaw. A heavy pressure will therefore be required on the appropriate rudder pedal.

manifold pressure are selected on the operating engine.

Select landing gear and flaps up.

Establish and/or maintain V_{yse}.

Note 1: If an engine fails when a missed approach is being carried out below Asymmetric Committal Height and prior to reaching the runway threshold, convert to a final approach and landing.

If an engine fails when a missed approach is being carried out after passing the runway threshold, consideration must be given to the aircraft's performance capability to safely climb away.

Note 2: In the case of airspeed being critical and insufficient height available to establish V_{yse}, or if height cannot be maintained after the aircraft is cleaned up, a controlled landing should be made in a clear area.

In the case of V_{yse} being attainable and a climb away achieved, continue the climb to a safe height and re-position the aircraft on the downwind leg.

Note 3: The ability to climb away from a low height when the airspeed is below V_{yse} will be vitally affected by the speed at which the pilot can correctly clean up the aircraft and complete the feathering drill.

In the event that the landing gear retraction system is operated from the inoperative engine then the effect of landing gear drag must be taken into account when making the decision to land or climb away.

COMPLETION STANDARDS

Upon the completion of this flight lesson the student must be capable of demonstrating his competence at handling engine failure situations at any stage during the take-off, circuit, approach and landing.

Additionally he should be able to maintain a selected airspeed within ± 5 knots and headings within ± 10° during simulated engine failure operations.

Finally, the student will need to appreciate that for each aircraft 'in a given Performance Group' there will be one combination of low height, low airspeed, high drag and high power at which it will not be possible to climb away should any one of these factors become more adverse when an engine fails near the ground.

Progress Tests

Progress Tests

This section contains a series of Progress Tests designed to enable you to test your level of knowledge in the subject material included in this manual. You should bear in mind the following points when completing the tests:

- They are designed to enable you to monitor your progress. Their objective is to provide a means whereby you can assess your knowledge and understanding at various stages in your learning task. If you can score good marks (75% or above) in these tests you will be able to complete your multi engine Rating oral examination with a high degree of confidence.

- The test items are not trick questions; each statement means exactly what it says. Therefore read each question, response or statement carefully and do not look for hidden meanings.

- Be sure that you understand what the test item asks, and then review the alternative responses. Following this, decide which response is the correct one, or work out the problem to obtain the correct answer.

- Always select the response which gives the most complete and correct answer; the others will be responses which are totally wrong, partially wrong or those which you might select if you lack sufficient knowledge of the subject.

- Upon completing each test, check your answers against those shown on page Q 36. Questions which give you difficulty or which you fail to answer correctly will give you an indication of those areas in which you lack understanding, and you should therefore review the appropriate parts of the subject before proceeding with your next stage of study.

Quiz No. 1

1 In relation to the pilot's responsibilities:

(a) Pre-Flight planning must include the selection of an alternate aerodrome.

(b) The aircraft's single engine ceiling must be taken into account when planning the intended and alternate routes.

(c) The selection of an alternate aerodrome is only an advisory recommendation.

(d) Both responses (a) and (b) are correct.

2 Which of the following responses is correct?:

(a) The loading options of a twin engined aeroplane are normally no greater than those of a single engined aeroplane.

(b) It is advisable to determine that a sufficient landing distance is available at the destination aerodrome, but this precaution is not mandatory.

(c) The loading options of a twin engined aeroplane are normally greater than those available for single engined aeroplanes.

(d) All of the above responses are incorrect.

3 For the purposes of pilot licensing aeroplanes are divided into Groups. In relation to a twin engined aeroplane:

(a) It may be classified in Group A or B.

(b) It will always be classified in Group B.

(c) It will usually be classified in Group A.

(d) It may be classified either in Group B or Group C.

4 In any applicable 13 month period, a pilot must have carried out a minimum number of flying hours in order to renew his certificate of experience. With reference to renewing a Group B Rating, which of the following is required?:

   (a)   A minimum of 3 hours dual and 2 hours 'in command' of a Group A aircraft.

   (b)   A minimum of 5 hours flying, of which one flight must have been in command of a multi engined aeroplane. Of this total, at least 3 hours must have been carried out 'in command'.

   (c)   5 hours dual in a Group B aeroplane.

   (d)   A minimum of 2 hours 'in command' and 3 hours dual in either a Group A or Group B aeroplane.

5 Which of the following responses is correct?:

   (a)   All flights undertaken in Group B aircraft must comply with the Weight and Performance requirements contained in the Air Navigation (General) Regulations.

   (b)   Group B aircraft do not have to be operated in compliance with the Articles contained in the Air Navigation Order.

   (c)   Compliance with the Weight and Performance requirements of the Air Navigation (General) Regulations is not mandatory for private flights.

   (d)   All the above responses are incorrect.

6 Aircraft certification procedures require multi engined aeroplanes to be divided into different 'Groups'. Which of the following responses defines the requirements for certification in Group C?:

   (a)   Aeroplanes with no specific provision for performance after engine failure.

   (b)   Aeroplanes with a performance level such that a forced landing should not be necessary if an engine fails after take-off and initial climb.

   (c)   Aeroplanes which have a minimum rate of climb of 500 fpm on one engine.

   (d)   None of the above responses is correct.

7 In order to obtain a multi engine Rating certain requirements must be met. In relation to these requirements which of the following responses is most correct?:

(a) It will be necessary to undertake a course of training conducted in accordance with a syllabus approved by the CAA.

(b) A flight test in a multi engined aeroplane must be completed. This flight test will cover all normal procedures and those emergency procedures which are applicable to the aircraft type.

(c) It will be necessary to obtain a pass in an oral examination conducted by an authorised PPL examiner.

(d) All the items in the above responses will be required.

8 The difference between performance information contained in Owner's Manuals/Pilot's Operating Handbooks and that contained in Flight Manuals is:

(a) Performance information in most Flight Manuals has been factored.

(b) Flight Manuals do not give information which allows for any small errors in pilot technique, or estimations in weight, temperature and wind velocity.

(c) Owner's Manuals contain factored performance information.

(d) Performance information obtained from most Flight Manuals is Gross Performance.

9 A pilot will need information relating to the aircraft he operates. This information should be obtained:

(a) Only from an approved Flight Manual.

(b) From the particular Manual designated in the Certificate of Airworthiness.

(c) From any Flight Manual relating to the particular model of aircraft.

(d) Only from a Pilot's Operating Handbook.

10 Which of the following responses are correct?:

(a) To comply with the regulations concerning Public Transport flights, any Flight Manual for the particular model of aircraft may be used.

(b) A Flight Manual is normally required for an aircraft to be placed in the Public Transport Category.

(c) In the case of some imported aeroplanes which have an English language Flight Manual approved by the CAA, a UK supplement will be issued and form part of the Flight Manual.

(d) Both responses (b) and (c) are correct.

ANSWER SHEET QUIZ NO. 1

Q	A
1	
2	
3	
4	
5	
6	
7	
8	
9	
10	

Quiz No. 2

1 The failure of one engine in a conventional twin engined aircraft will result in:

(a) A reduction in total lift and drag.

(b) An asymmetry of thrust and a reduction in drag.

(c) An asymmetry of thrust and drag and a reduction in total lift.

(d) No change in the basic forces provided sufficient airspeed is maintained.

2 The *primary* factor affecting a pilot's ability to control a twin engined aircraft following the failure of one engine is:

(a) Altitude.

(b) Aircraft configuration.

(c) Airspeed.

(d) The position of the centre of gravity.

3 Which of the following responses is correct?:

(a) The term 'critical engine' is used to describe the engine which if failed will lead to the largest yawing moment for a given set of conditions.

(b) The closer the engines are placed to the aircraft's centre-line the greater will be the yawing moment from the operating engine when flying on asymmetric power.

(c) The term 'critical engine' will only apply to a conventional twin engined aircraft if it has propellers which rotate in opposite directions.

(d) None of the above responses is correct.

4   The distance required to bring a multi engined aircraft to a stop relative to a single engined aircraft when a take-off is aborted will be:

(a)   Less.

(b)   About the same.

(c)   Significantly greater.

(d)   None of the above responses is correct.

5   If one engine fails during flight the aircraft will immediately:

(a)   Yaw towards the direction of the failed engine if climbing power is being used.

(b)   Roll in the direction of the failed engine.

(c)   Yaw towards the direction of the operating engine if less than climbing power is being used.

(d)   Both responses (a) and (b) are correct.

6   If the 'critical engine' fails:

(a)   The aircraft will be unable to maintain altitude.

(b)   The yawing moment will be greater than if the opposite engine had failed.

(c)   The power of the operating engine will need to be reduced if directional control is to be maintained.

(d)   All the above responses are correct.

7   In relation to the residual side forces produced as a result of single engined flight, which of the following responses is correct:

(a)   If rudder is used to prevent yaw the side forces will be eliminated.

(b)   If sufficient rudder deflection is being used to maintain a constant direction, the side forces will be balanced out and the aircraft's longitudinal axis will be aligned exactly along the line of flight.

(c)   Although the use of rudder may result in the side forces being balanced out, it will not be possible to centre the ball of the balance indicator.

(d)   At normal cruising airspeeds the side forces can be balanced out, but the aircraft's longitudinal axis will be slightly offset from the line of flight.

8 If an engine fails in a conventional twin engined aircraft, the windmilling drag from the propeller of the inoperative engine:

 (a) Will cause a significant increase in the total drag.

 (b) Will be extremely small and have no effect upon the aircraft's performance.

 (c) Will tend to offset the yaw produced from the thrust of the operating engine.

 (d) Both responses (b) and (c) are correct.

9 Use of bank towards the operating engine during single engined flight will assist directional control when the aircraft is flying at a low airspeed. In this situation:

 (a) The ball of the balance indicator will be in the centre although a slight yaw will be taking place.

 (b) The higher the airspeed the greater will be the required angle of bank.

 (c) The ball of the balance indicator will be in the centre although a small sideslip will be present.

 (d) The greater the angle of bank, the further will be the ball from its central position.

10 If the right engine is inoperative and cruising airspeed is being maintained:

 (a) It will be easier to control a turn to the left.

 (b) It will be easier to control a turn to the right.

 (c) Control of turns in either direction will be the same.

 (d) All the above responses are incorrect.

ANSWER SHEET QUIZ NO. 2

Q	A
1	
2	
3	
4	
5	
6	
7	
8	
9	
10	

Quiz No. 3

1 In relation to controlling the aircraft during asymmetric flight at single engine cruising speed, which of the following responses is correct?:

   (a) The pilot should be careful to avoid a situation where directional control is obtained through the use of too much aileron and insufficient rudder.

   (b) The rudder should be used to prevent yaw, in conjunction with the minimum amount of aileron deflection to keep the wings laterally level.

   (c) For a fixed power setting the elevators should be used to control airspeed.

   (d) All the above responses are correct.

2 In relation to the failure of one engine, if the critical engine fails and a constant speed is maintained:

   (a) A larger rudder deflection will be needed to combat the yaw.

   (b) A smaller rudder deflection will be needed to combat the yaw.

   (c) The single engined performance will be less.

   (d) Both responses (a) and (c) are correct.

3 The effective force obtained from the use of rudder:

   (a) Is not affected by the position of the centre of gravity provided it is within its permitted range.

   (b) Is reduced with a forward movement of the centre of gravity.

   (c) Is increased with a rearward movement of the centre of gravity.

   (d) Is reduced with a rearward movement of the centre of gravity.

4 Which of the following responses most correctly defines the conditions under which V_{mca} is established?:

(a) Full take-off power on the operating engine.
The rearmost allowable centre of gravity.
The flaps in the take-off position.
A minimum rate of climb of 100 fpm.
The landing gear retracted.
The propeller of the inoperative engine windmilling in the fine pitch position.

(b) Full take-off power on the critical engine.
The flaps set in the take-off position.
The landing gear extended.
The propeller of the inoperative engine windmilling in fine pitch.
A calculated 'mean' position of the centre of gravity.

(c) Full take-off power on the operating engine.
The rearmost allowable centre of gravity.
The flaps in the take-off position.
The landing gear extended.
The propeller of the inoperative engine in the fine pitch position.

(d) Full take-off power on the operating engine.
The rearmost allowable centre of gravity.
The landing gear retracted.
The propeller of the inoperative engine windmilling in the fine pitch position.
Flaps set in the take-off position.

5 In the case of an aircraft with normally aspirated engines:

(a) The indicated V_{mc} will increase as altitude is gained.

(b) The indicated V_{mc} will decrease as altitude is gained.

(c) The indicated V_{mc} will remain the same regardless of altitude.

(d) None of the above responses is correct.

6 If one engine fails on a twin engined aircraft, the power available will be reduced by 50%. In these circumstances the '*excess thrust horsepower available*' could be reduced to approximately:

   (a)   70%.

   (b)   Between 10% and 20% of the normal both engines operating figure.

   (c)   60%.

   (d)   80%.

7 In relation to light twin engined aircraft certificated in Performance Group C or E, these aircraft are:

   (a)   Required to demonstrate their ability to climb on one engine at a rate of at least 100 fpm.

   (b)   Not required to demonstrate any climb performance capability on one engine.

   (c)   Required to have a stalling speed in excess of V_{mca}.

   (d)   Both responses (a) and (c) are correct.

8 When determining a practical single engine ceiling for a particular aircraft type:

   (a)   The Critical Altitude should be used.

   (b)   The single engine Absolute Ceiling as shown in the aircraft manual should be used.

   (c)   The figure which relates to the single engine Service Ceiling is the most sensible one to use.

   (d)   The altitude at which the rate of climb (at V_{yse}) is reduced to 150 fpm should be used.

9 The abbreviations TODA and LDA as shown in the AGA Section of the UK Air Pilot are defined as:

   (a)   Take-off and landing run available in relation to the particular runway.

   (b)   Take-off distance and landing run available at the particular aerodrome.

   (c)   Take-off distance and landing distance available in relation to the particular runway.

   (d)   Both responses (a) and (c) are correct.

10 In relation to the take-off procedure after lift off, which of the following responses is correct?:

(a) Allow the speed to build up quickly by flying level with the ground until the speed is in excess of V_y.

(b) Gain height as quickly as possible by climbing at a speed below V_x.

(c) Gain height as quickly as possible by climbing at a speed below V_{xse}.

(d) Initially maintain maximum permitted power and climb at not less than V_{yse} and not more than V_y.

ANSWER SHEET QUIZ NO. 3

Q	A
1	
2	
3	
4	
5	
6	
7	
8	
9	
10	

CONVERSION TO TWIN ENGINED AIRCRAFT

Quiz No. 4

The following questions relate to your training aircraft and to obtain the answers you will need to refer to the aircraft manual.

1   Based on the following data, determine whether the all up weight and centre of gravity are within limits:

Pilot and front passenger   ...   ...   85 kg ea
First row of passenger seats (2 passengers)   85 kg ea
Fuel load   ...   .   Full tanks
Baggage (rear location)   ...   ...   90 kg

Yes/No ....

2   Give one power setting which produces 75% power at 5000' with an outside air temperature of 10°C:

Manifold pressure ....
rpm   ....

3   What is the maximum range with full fuel tanks, zero wind and the maximum permitted all up weight (select maximum range altitude)?:

Nautical miles ....

4   What is the maximum endurance of your aircraft in the following conditions?:

Altitude 5000'.
Maximum fuel.
Maximum permitted all up weight.

Hours/Minutes ....

5   What is the normal fuel flow (or fuel pressure) during take-off at maximum permitted power from an aerodrome at sea level?:

....

6   On what occasions should the electric fuel pumps be switched on?:

   ....
   ....
   ....

7   Where is the 'Alternate Static Source' and how is it operated?:

   ....
   ....
   ....

8   Describe the correct 'Mixture Leaning Technique' for your aircraft:

   ....
   ....
   ....

9   Describe the method of operating the landing gear 'Emergency Lowering' system:

   ....
   ....
   ....

10   Draw a simple line diagram of your aircraft fuel system and list details (if applicable) of any restrictions in fuel management:

Quiz No. 5

The following questions relate to your training aircraft and to obtain the answers you will need to refer to the aircraft manual.

1 What is V_y at mean sea level?:   Answer ....

2 What is V_{yse} at mean sea level?:   Answer ....

3 What is V_x at mean sea level?:   Answer ....

4 What are the maximum speeds for lowering the flaps and landing gear?:
                                             Answer V_{fe} ....
                                                    V_{lo} ....

5 What is V_{mca}?:   Answer ....

6 What is the Safety Speed (V_2)?:   Answer ....

7 What is the stalling speed of the aircraft at maximum all up weight, clean configuration, no power and a load factor of 1?:
                                             Answer ....

8 What will be the stalling speed under the same conditions but with full flap and landing gear lowered?:
                                             Answer ....

9 By how much would you expect the stalling speed to increase during a 45° level steep turn?:
                                             Answer ....

10 What is the maximum permitted power during take-off?:
                                             Manifold pressure ....
                                             rpm   ....

Quiz No. 6

The following questions relate to your training aircraft and to obtain the answers you will need to refer to the aircraft manual.

1 Compute the take-off distance for your aircraft under the following conditions:

Maximum permitted all up weight.

Pressure Altitude	...	...	...	2000'
Air Temperature	...	...	...	25°C
Wind Component	...	...	...	10 knots

Answer .... metres

2 Using the same conditions described in question 1, what is the required landing distance:

Answer .... metres

3 Compute the take-off run for your aircraft under the following conditions:

Maximum permitted all up weight.

Pressure Altitude	...	...	...	1500'
Air Temperature	...	...	...	20°C
Wind	...	...	...	260/30
Take-Off Runway	...	...	...	22

Answer .... metres

4 Using the same conditions described in question 3, work out the length of the landing run:

Answer .... metres

5   List the procedure to adopt in case of an engine fire during flight:

....
....
....
....

6   List the emergency descent procedure:

....
....

7   What is the time (approximately) in seconds for the landing gear to lower?:

Answer ....

8   What is the correct initial approach speed in normal conditions?:

Answer ....

9   What is the correct 'runway threshold speed' in normal conditions?:

Answer ....

10   List the procedure to adopt in the event of a cabin fire:

....
....
....
....

Quiz No. 7

Questions 1 to 4 relate to your training aircraft and to obtain the answers you will need to refer to the aircraft manual.

1 The tachometer will always clearly indicate which engine has failed. True or False?

                                        Answer ....

2 Using the information shown on page 65, work out the single engine *excess thrust horsepower* available from your training aircraft:

                                        Answer ....

3 What is the recommended power setting to obtain 'zero thrust' for sea level under standard atmospheric conditions?:

                                        Answer ....

4 What are the best engine instruments to use when confirming a particular engine has failed during flight?:

                                        Answer ....
                                        ....
                                        ....

5 If the 'inside engine' fails during a level turn the aircraft will tend to roll out of the turn. True or False?

                                        Answer ....

6 If an aircraft yaws due to engine failure whilst in level flight at cruising power, the balance indicator will move towards the operating engine. True or False?

                                        Answer ....

7   Assuming the left engine fails during cruising flight, which of the following responses is correct:

   (a)   You will need to apply pressure on the left rudder pedal to maintain directional control. The ailerons should then be held in the neutral position.

   (b)   You will need to apply pressure on the left rudder pedal and raise the right aileron to maintain directional control.

   (c)   You will need to apply pressure on the right rudder pedal whilst keeping the ailerons in the neutral position.

   (d)   Pressure will have to be applied to the right rudder pedal and the ailerons should be used to keep the wings laterally level.

8   If the left engine fails during cruising flight and no corrective action is taken, the aircraft will:

   (a)   Yaw and roll to the left, followed by a spiral descent.

   (b)   Yaw and roll to the right, followed by a spiral descent.

   (c)   Maintain its original heading for a few seconds and then yaw and roll to the right.

   (d)   All the above responses are incorrect.

9   If during cruising flight the right engine partially fails and the pilot closes the left throttle whilst attempting to maintain a constant direction, he will need to use:

   (a)   Additional left rudder.

   (b)   Less right rudder.

   (c)   Less left rudder.

   (d)   More right rudder.

10 Which of the following responses is correct:

  (a) If the left engine fails during a level turn, the aircraft will yaw and roll to the left and rapidly enter a spiral descent.

  (b) If an engine fails during a descent at low power in turbulent weather conditions, it may be difficult to immediately detect that engine failure has occurred.

  (c) Following an engine failure, the most pronounced yaw will occur during climbing flight at low airspeed and maximum power.

  (d) All the above responses are correct.

ANSWER SHEET QUIZ NO. 7

Q	A
7	
8	
9	
10	

Quiz No. 8

Question 1 relates to your training aircraft and to obtain the answer you will need to refer to the aircraft manual.

1 Does the failure of one engine affect the landing gear, flaps or electrical systems? If so, nominate the appropriate system and engine:

System	Engine	
	Right	Left
Landing Gear		
Flaps		
Electric		

2 What airspeed will give the maximum rate of climb or minimum rate of descent with one propeller feathered?:

(a) V_{mca}.

(b) V_{sse}.

(c) V_{yse}.

(d) V_{xse}.

3   What is the best course of action if an engine fails during take-off and before V_{mca} is achieved?:

(a)   Maintain direction, reduce drag to a minimum and continue to accelerate to V_2.·

(b)   Immediately close both throttles and abandon the take-off.

(c)   Maintain directional control and attempt to remedy the failure.

(d)   Reduce power on the operating engine and if sufficient runway remains continue until V_2 is achieved, following which lift off can be made and V_{yse} obtained.

4   If an engine fails when the aircraft is in flight at an airspeed below V_{mc}, the first action apart from attempting to maintain direction with the rudder should be:

(a)   Immediately increase the power to maximum.

(b)   Open both throttles to the full power position.

(c)   Partially close both throttles whilst lowering the aircraft's nose to gain airspeed as quickly as possible.

(d)   Leave both throttles open and feather the propeller of the failed engine.

5   Positive confirmation of which engine has failed should be established by:

(a)   The engine instrument readings.

(b)   The direction of heading change.

(c)   Gradually closing the throttle of the engine suspected of failing.

(d)   Bringing one rpm lever fully back.

6   During a single engine climb following an engine failure immediately after take-off:

(a)   The correct airspeed to achieve is V_{yse}.

(b)   Flap and landing gear should be raised as soon as possible compatible with safety.

(c)   The cowl flaps on the failed engine should be closed to the minimum drag position.

(d)   All the above responses are correct.

7 During a single engined approach:

(a) The rpm lever of the operating engine should be in the fully forward position.

(b) It will be advisable to maintain at least V_{yse} until the Asymmetric Committal Height is reached.

(c) The decision to descend below Asymmetric Committal Height should only be taken if:
ATC have given a clearance to land.
The landing gear is locked down.
The runway is clear, and the aircraft is in a suitable position to complete the final stage of the approach.

(d) All the above responses are correct.

8 Immediately after closing the throttle of the operating engine during a single engined landing:

(a) There will be a yaw towards the feathered engine.

(b) There will be a yaw towards the operating engine.

(c) No yaw will occur.

(d) All the above responses are incorrect.

9 If an engine fails below Asymmetric Committal Height during a normal approach with both engines operating:

(a) A go round again should be implemented.

(b) The approach to landing should be continued.

(c) Any attempt to land must first be cleared by ATC.

(d) All the above responses are incorrect.

10 When an engine fails at low height following take-off, the throttle and rpm levers should be checked fully forward. The purpose of this action is to ensure that:

(a) The maximum power will be available to operate the ancillary systems.

(b) A high oil pressure on the operating engine is maintained.

(c) Maximum power is being used from the operating engine until the pilot has had the opportunity to determine which engine has failed.

(d) To assist in the identification of the failed engine.

ANSWER SHEET QUIZ NO. 8

Q	A
2	
3	
4	
5	
6	
7	
8	
9	
10	

Quiz No. 9

Questions 1 to 7 relate to your training aircraft and to obtain the answers you will need to refer to the aircraft manual.

1 In what order should the rpm, throttle and mixture control levers be moved when feathering a propeller?:

Answer 1. ....

2. ....

3. ....

2 If the engine fails, will it be possible to run the operating engine from the left (main) fuel tank?:

Answer ....

3 How many fuel strainer valves is your aircraft equipped with?:

Answer ....

4 Can the fuel crossfeed system be used during take-off or landing?:

Answer ....

5 Which is the 'critical' engine (if applicable to your aircraft)?:

Answer ....

6 During take-off following a 'touch and go' landing, what is the correct sequence for power application and drag reduction?:

Answer 1 .... 2 ....

7   What device is used to prevent inadvertent retraction of the landing gear during ground operations, and under what circumstances could this device fail to prevent an inadvertent retraction?

....

....

....

8   In relation to the use of bank to assist directional control during single engined flight, which of the following responses is correct?:

(a)   The use of bank will only be necessary when the airspeed is high and the operating engine is developing more than 75% power.

(b)   Bank will be required if the airspeed is above V_{yse} and moderate power is being used on the operating engine.

(c)   Bank, applied towards the operating engine, should be used when the airspeed is low and high power is being used.

(d)   The use of bank towards the operating engine is unlikely to be required when the airspeed is low and high power is being developed from the operating engine.

9   In the event of one engine failing during flight, your first action should be to:

(a)   Maintain directional and lateral control.

(b)   Identify the failed engine.

(c)   Reduce drag to a minimum.

(d)   Determine the cause of failure.

10 In relation to Asymmetric Committal Height:

(a) Its use will be unnecessary if the aircraft is capable of climbing on one engine.

(b) It need only be nominated when operating at all up weight.

(c) This height should be sufficient to ensure that:
. . . following the application of full power on the operating engine, a safe height will still obtain whilst drag is being reduced and the aircraft established in a climb. In deciding this height, consideration must also be given to the height of any obstructions along the climb out path . . .

(d) None of the above responses applies.

ANSWER SHEET QUIZ NO. 9

Q	A
8	
9	
10	

Answers to Progress Tests

QUIZ No 1	
1	d
2	b
3	d
4	b
5	c
6	d
7	d
8	a
9	b
10	d

QUIZ No 2	
1	c
2	c
3	a
4	c
5	d
6	b
7	d
8	a
9	d
10	b

QUIZ No 3	
1	d
2	d
3	d
4	d
5	b
6	b
7	b
8	c
9	c
10	d

QUIZ No 7	
5	False
6	True
7	d
8	a
9	c
10	d

QUIZ No 8	
2	c
3	b
4	c
5	c
6	d
7	d
8	b
9	b
10	c

QUIZ No 9	
8	c
9	a
10	c